Primal Mothering In A Modern World

by

Hygeia Halfmoon, Ph.D.

Published by
Maul Brothers Publishing
San Diego, California

What people are saying about **Primal Mothering**:

"I read your book like a woman-companion who shares my same inner-voice and from whom I can learn even more. Your words are so strong and yet so simple — I mean, it's what we ALL really know already and have inside of us; we just don't know how to listen anymore."

"Thank you so much for your book. I couldn't put it down, I laughed and cried along with you and came in touch with my own feelings of anger and loss of power when I put my trust in a midwife and was betrayed during the final moments. Your book should be required reading for women of today as it touches on many, many core issues in a delightful way."

"I was inspired and touched by your honesty and humanness. I feel there's hope for me now, even with setbacks. Also, I feel validated about having my daughter sleep in bed between her dad and me. Thanks!"

"Your book is brilliant — I couldn't put it down. You wrote a book that really needed to be written, as I'm sure lots of readers will gain inspiration and courage from reading it just as I did. It really gave me a boost reading it and reminded me to focus my life and use all the energy and inspiration that is in the world."

"Thanks for your book! My family nibbled around the edges, then slowly savored every bite of this Primal Mothering fare. Our family of 'free-lance' autodidacts especially enjoyed the chapter on home-schooling."

"I opened your book and I just started reading and halfway through the first paragraph, my heart was rejoicing."

"Your book is so intimately done, so on the mark of excellent writing — a real courageous book that should be in every apartment, every home in the USA, and the world for that matter. Such courage on your part. Bless you, Bless you, Bless you."

"Primal Mothering isn't just a book that pregnant women should read. It is a book for a breast-starved population. The empowerment I've received from reading your book has enabled me to move away from the negative thinking patterns that used to affect my everyday decision-making."

"As a child and parenting counselor, I can confidently say that if children were united with their mother the way Nature designed it for them, we would see no crime, corruption, self destructiveness, or war. Hygeia Halfmoon has a gift to give which no money can ever pay back. In her personal life, she broke the chain of violence and control, and has already passed the torch to many other parents through her writing and speaking."

"Through my own vast nationwide experience with parents, I can assure you that parents are ready for this message. With no support in the media and society at large, many parents deny their own feelings and follow the common advice of separation in childrearing. However, when given the validation to their feelings, they often jump on the 'Reunion' wagon with all their heart. This is why we need people like Hygeia Halfmoon to carry her most important message out into the world."

Other Books By Hygeia Halfmoon:

Anatomy Of An Accomplishment
Cooked Foods Anonymous
Everyday Erotica For The Totally Devoted Couple
Highway To Health: A Call To Fruitarianism
I Can Do This! An Unassisted Childbirth
Experiential Guide
Love Letters
Prostitute To Ph.D.: Graduating From Sexual Dysfunction
Raw-Food Recipes: A Fruitarian Child's Delight!
Wealth Is The Answer

Primal Mothering In A Modern World
By Hygeia Halfmoon, Ph.D.

Disclaimer:
This book is not intended as medical, obstetric, or pediatric advice because Hygeia Halfmoon does not recommend the use of standard birthing procedures, nor does she advocate the use of cooked foods or medicines to alleviate health challenges. Because there is always some risk involved, the author, publisher, and/or distributors of this book are not responsible for any adverse consequences or detoxification effects resulting from the use of any birthing procedures or dietary suggestions described hereafter.

Second Edition: April 20, 1998

Front Cover: Raw-Foodists Jennifer Vanlaanen-Smit and Erik Smit are pictured with their two exuberant children.
Cover Art: Ken Seaney, Ground Zero Graphic Design
Cover Design: David Wolfe
Text Layout: Stephen Arlin, Ken Seaney

Printed in North America by
Maul Brothers Publishing
PO Box 900202
San Diego, CA 92190 USA
(619) 645-7282

ISBN #0-9653533-4-6

DEDICATION

To Jody Lee who, like Maynard Gull, learned that she has the freedom to be herself, her true self, here and now, and nothing can stand in her way.

Acknowledgments

This book represents the individual dreams of every person who has ever crossed my path...T.C. Fry's dream for a curriculum addressing Natural Mothering; David Wolfe's dream to publish a book about Fruitarian Mothering; Laura Kaplan Shanley's dream to awaken women to the joys of sovereign birth; Les Brown's dream to encourage people to live their dreams; Susan Jeffer's dream to teach the art of feeling the fear and doing it anyway; Betsy Corwin's dream to help the people she loves to become happy, joyous, and free; Cheryl Young's dream to raise her children according to the dictates of her heart; and the dreams of my children — dreams which are unfolding for the simple fact that my mothering skills have been so gracefully influenced by every person who has ever crossed my path.

Table of Contents

x

"We know nothing 'til intuition agrees." — Richard Bach

Chapter 1

PRIMAL MOTHERING
Birthing A New Humanity

"Women have millions of years of genetically-encoded intelligences, intuitions, capacities, knowledges, powers, and cellular knowings of exactly what to do with the infant."
— **Joseph Chilton Pearce**

The modern world has made a token of the word "natural." In fact, very little of modern humanity could be described as natural. Just because modern living and thinking practices are prevalent and therefore considered normal, that doesn't mean they are natural.

Thus, I have chosen the term "primal" as opposed to "natural" to refer to the innate wisdom which transcends transitory theories and maintains its integrity, despite the trends of the day. No matter what is done to the tree, it is the tree's roots which will ensure its future. And so it is with primal mothering, for its roots will save humanity when the storms of social trial and error have stripped all but the infinite wisdom which rests securely in female intellect.

This book is a wake-up call aimed at stirring your primal knowledge about mothering. The ideas you read about in this book are neither prevalent nor are they normal. In fact, they smell of heresy to those interested in maintaining the status quo. However, if your mothering instincts scream silently in pain while your actions hesitatingly follow in the wake of social consciousness, then I hope to bring you home to yourself. If, for instance, you are frustrated by society's message that, in these busy, modern times, children are expected to be neither seen nor heard; if you wonder why the physically-challenged minority in our society have been heard to the tune of public access, while mothers — being a majority — continue to struggle with over-sized toilet seats for their young in public bathrooms, NO KIDS/NO PETS rental ads in newspapers, and a host of other discriminations, this book is for you. Yes, this book is radical. These guiding principles represent the roots of mothering — that place of entrance where nutrients converge to feed the tree in its entirety. Black Elk once delivered a message which reminds us, "It may be that some little root of the sacred tree still lives. Nourish it then, that it may leaf and bloom and fill with singing birds." Though buried deeply from view in this modern age, the instincts of women are alive nonetheless. One layer at a time, we will find ourselves again and, in doing so, we will put humanity back on track. We will once again be free to be our true selves, teachers of love to a species so easily led astray.

With the courage to admit, accept, and embrace our position as primal mothers, we automatically become recipients of inner peace as the little girl of us merges with our womanhood. Primal mothering is like walking barefoot in a meadow of wild-flowers. It brings us alive, awakens us from the dismal dreari-ness of social consciousness, and relieves us of the guilt and remorse which so often accompany decisions based in compro-mise. Primal mothering touches our soul in a way that modern mothering methods cannot. Primal mothering makes powerful women out of us because we flex muscles which otherwise atro-phy in the name of social acceptance. We question authority, and then become the authors of our own mothering careers, our own lives. By defending Nature, we guarantee our children their right to a natural unfolding.

This is not a text-book of intellectual theory, but rather, an invocation of what you already know. But the paradox with instincts is that, though we are born with them, we must be exposed to the daily rhythm of their reality in order to activate and maintain that knowledge within ourselves. For instance, if women around us are not breastfeeding or bonding with their young, the wake-up call to our own primal mothering is muffled and we can easily fall prey to such practices as bottle-feeding and mother-infant separation.

We must silence the social chatter so we may hear the different drummer, the urge in our hearts which cries "mother and child togetherness." I am reminded of the story **Jonathan Livingston Seagull** where it was said, "He spoke of very simple things, that it is right for a gull to fly, that freedom is the very nature of his being, that whatever stands against that freedom must be set aside, be it ritual or superstition or limitation in any form."

Listening to ourselves and then taking action on the wisdom from within can be a scary endeavor as we become vulnerable to attack by family members, husbands, friends, religious leaders, medical workers, and others who disagree with us. Laura Kaplan Shanley, author of **Unassisted Childbirth** writes, "When we decide to take our lives into our own hands, we must be prepared to encounter resistance. There will always be those who believe we are not qualified to do so." Opposition strikes when we least expect it, and it is only conviction to our instincts which pulls us through moments of social disapproval.

One afternoon, while pushing a cart through the produce section of my neighborhood grocery store, the manager looked up and, upon noticing my baby tucked securely against me in a baby sling barked, "Hey, why don't you put your baby in the front of the cart where she belongs?" I said that she was fine and happy to be next to me, to which he replied, "Spoiled baby!" I was holding a bunch of overly-ripe bananas as he spoke those words, raised them to his face, and showed him the true definition of spoiled.

According to Webster's Dictionary, spoil means "to harm severely, to ruin, to impair the quality of, to become unfit for use." When people tell us we are spoiling our young, in the very moment that we are adhering to our mothering instincts and giving them exactly what they need, we are torn between their "expert" opinion and our innate knowing. Unfortunately, one criticism can throw us off and leave us questioning virtually every aspect of our mothering career. It takes a great deal of conscious contact with our primal intuition to hold steady in times of judgment. We all know fruit only spoils when it is neglected, when it is left to rot, when it is not enjoyed fully at the ripe stage. Looking back at this definition of spoiled, could that more accurately be describing the sad results of children who have not been raised under the wing of a primal mother?

Primal mothering is an adventure in commitment. It leads us through corridors past, present, and future. I cringe when, during times of guiding my children, I hear myself sound like my parents. When this happens, I commit to the inner healing necessary for me to erase those unhealthy parenting tapes learned from my own past. I rise to the occasions of the present, knowing the power to handle all situations resides in me. And I celebrate my role in the future, where all of my efforts will be played out in the generations to come.

Societal disapproval is something we must become immune to as we draw nearer to the gentle prodding of our mothering instincts. Social pressure may be applied by family members, husbands, friends, neighbors, community leaders, churches, medical authorities, state laws, government policy, and — even worse — our own minds due to all this cultural conditioning. Taking flight means to loosen our burdens by learning to obey our hearts while turning down the volume on society. Whether overt or covert, there's always somebody who challenges our determination to self-govern.

I remember the time I gave my power away to a police officer. One night, while seven months pregnant, I had a tire blow-out on the way home. I pulled over and, without benefit of flashlight, began the challenging task of trusting myself to change my own tire. A policeman drove up just as I was loosening the last lug nut, preparing to feel the victory of my efforts. I kindly refused his offer of help, but HE refused to honor my decision to fix the tire myself. My personal goal finally gave way to his authoritarian insistence...he finished changing the tire.

When he drove off, I felt ripped off. A challenge designed to empower me had fizzled down to concern for the macho image of a uniformed cop. Given my lifelong lessons in social obedience and protecting the male ego, it's no wonder that I couldn't muster up the courage to send that police officer on his way.

This obedience to authority is especially practiced by women in the realm of medicine. Doctors tell us what to do, when to do it, how long to do it, and when to stop. It's a pelvic gold-mine for medical profiteers, guised in the belief that we, as women, know next-to-nothing about meeting the needs of our pregnancies, our births, our babies, and the ongoing needs of our young.

On Easter morning twelve years ago, I enacted my own ascension by deciding to take back my life and my health. I discarded my servile behavior and walked away from an existence previously controlled by societal pressure. What next? I felt free, but fragile. After all, I had not been conditioned to think for myself, to listen to my innermost voice, or to trust my instincts. I began a search for the answers to my questions. I left college and traveled south until I happened upon the poverty-stricken sidewalks of a Mexican village where I nearly tripped over a mother who was sitting on the curb nursing her young.

In front of this mother/child couple rested an old tin can serving as a collection plate to be hopefully filled by generous passers-by. When I put a quarter into that can and heard the clinking sound of metal against metal, I suddenly awoke from a deep sleep which had defined my life experience up to that point. In that moment, my mission in life stared me in the face as the song "Mother and Child Reunion" floated gently across my psyche. I was observing human symbiosis; mother needing baby as much as baby needs mother.

This lesson in mother-child interaction stayed with me to serve as a cornerstone when, just one year later, while walking down a sidewalk, not in Mexico but Oklahoma, my then-husband insisted I put our newborn into day-care so I could go back to work. With the vehemence of a she-bear, I growled back at him, "I will stand on this street-corner collecting coins before putting my baby in day-care!" Twelve years and three children later, I'm still committed to obeying my heart and my "tin can" is always within reach, should I need it.

I always keep my eye on the mark, that place in time years down the road when I will look back and feel good about my mothering decisions. Five years ago, in the midst of a natural disaster, I was given the opportunity to take inventory and determine if intuitive integrity had indeed ruled my choices in mothering. Hurricane Iniki swept over our small island of Kauai like the hand of destruction in a hurry and, with children in my arms and the roof ready to fly, death seemed a near certainty. Rising above the fear and anguish, like a phoenix from the ashes, came the scent of sweet serenity embracing me, as it had for the poverty-stricken mother I saw in that tiny Mexican village a decade prior. I had honored my mothering instincts at every turn, and regret did not accompany me in these supposed final moments of life.

When we tend to the needs of our young we are, in fact, nurturing ourselves. We have the great benefit of feeling good about who we have been for our children. Primal mothering is its own reward. Turning inside ourselves, over and over again with each choice we make, our convictions lead us to levels of serenity which no amount of materialism or social approval can reach. Following our hearts comes more easily when we have an understanding of the social myths surrounding mothering; myths which have silenced our souls up until now. In returning to the realness that exists inside the world of primal mothering, we can see the ridiculousness of these myths which have been driving women away from their heartfelt knowledge for too many years now.

One myth which reflects "modern" choices in mothering, as opposed to the primal touch, is the idea that children are expensive. Building the financial bank account prior to conception is fine, but certainly not a prerequisite to entering motherhood. If we wait for all the conditions to be right, we may not get started onto our path of mothering when we intuitively hear the call. When we break free from following social beliefs that otherwise lead to doctor and hospital bills, plastic carrying devices, baby furniture, infant formula, jarred baby food, disposable diapers, and day-care, we are freed-up to look with enthusiasm to the glowing benefits of being with and raising the children who come through us rather than grappling with finances. Primal mothering offers equal biological rights to children born into rags or riches. Outwitting poverty comes easy for those of us viewing life choices from the context of true need, thus minimizing daily stress and teaching healthy human values to our offspring.

Swimming upstream against social consciousness is indeed challenging, but the paradox of upstream mothering is that the elements of it are downstream and easy. For instance, forgetting formula feedings and instead engaging our milk-producing breasts makes the difference between the chore of preparing bottles in the middle of the night — not to mention having to hold the bottle upright until our babies are finished and cleaning the bottles come morning — or pulling our infants closer to nurse at our breasts without either ourselves or our babies having to come fully awake.

For many women in our society who want to raise children, waiting for all the conditions to be right includes the notion "First comes love, then comes marriage, then comes baby in a baby carriage." In truth, at least one third of all babies in our culture are born out-of-wedlock, and fully half of American mothers are raising their children single-handed. Prior to my career in mothering, I was frightened at the idea of single parenting. But I soon realized a clash was taking place between my mothering instincts and the expectations which existed inside my marriage. I had to make a decision. I decided single parenting was a necessary step toward my deepening commitment to primal mothering, and soon realized it was far more soul-enriching to raise my child without a partner than it was to lose sight of my mothering instincts for the sake of appeasing a man.

As is always the case with following my heart, primal mothering has been my ticket to personal growth. Codependency recovery has followed each decision that embraced my mothering instincts. I've had to learn the art of nurturing myself and meeting the needs of my children instead of automatically and obligingly taking care of a man. I've had to steal away in the middle of the night to enter the nearest women's shelter because I finally agreed it's not acceptable to be hit and verbally abused by my partner. And, while in those women's shelters, I've watched the way mothers feel guilty for tending to their own needs, and feel confused about what their children's needs really are. I have also seen how unimportant those combined needs are to many authority figures.

One night, a young woman entered the back kitchen door of that women's shelter — bruised and bleeding — with both a newborn and a toddler dangling from her weary arms. After helping her lull those beautiful babies to sleep, we helped her to calm down. She began to feel the safety of the shelter. As she sipped a warm cup of tea and soothed herself with a deep heaving cry, the phone in the hallway began to ring. It was the police headquarters. The officers were upset because this woman's husband — the man who had beat her just an hour prior — was ranting and raving in the police station, demanding to know where his wife was and refusing to leave. When the shelter staff member explained the young woman's recent abusive experience, the officer coldly replied, "Well, tell her to get ready to leave because we're on our way to get her. We're not going to have this guy causing trouble around here all night!"

Less than fifteen minutes later, uniformed policemen were at that supposedly safe kitchen door and the battered woman grabbed up her sleeping babies and obediently left the shelter, only to head back out into the storm of domestic violence.

Domestic violence is deadly. More women die at the hands of their partners than from any other fatality. For many more, their plight doesn't show up in the statistics because the scars don't necessarily show on the surface of their bodies. Emotional abuse is the internal injury of domestic violence. Women must become empowered enough to first identify the abuse and defend themselves by seeking an environment of physical safety, then learn to avoid relationships and situations which are non-supportive of both their needs and the needs of their young. We may need to accept the reality that a generation or two of children will be fatherless, as each gender faces and follows through with necessary healing for healthy human interactions.

Addiction recovery, breaking past codependency issues, inner child healing — these are the tools which light the way to a future of healthier family systems. Until then, the primal mothering needs of our young continue to exist and we can embrace this responsibility with a sense of determination and pride.

Because so many women find themselves struggling to get free from relationship dysfunction, a growing percentage of mothers and children are financially dependent on government programs. Welfare reform is an important step toward building healthier families, but not the kind of reform we so often hear about. Getting mothers out into the work-force and babies into daycare does not nurture the seeds of mother/child togetherness. I propose that welfare reform consist of leading women to recovery from dysfunctional relationships via methods in both personal counseling and group support, as well as instilling the art of financial independence by developing entrepreneurial skills for creating home businesses, and guaranteed business loans for implementing those businesses, thus protecting and honoring the mother/child bond. In my book **Anatomy Of An Accomplishment**, I touch more in-depth upon the need to tap into our deeper talents and develop a financial base derived from those talents without sacrificing the primal needs of our children.

For much of my mothering career I elected to use the welfare system according to the vision I saw for myself and my family. I gratefully accepted public assistance while at the same time working diligently on my codependency recovery, developing my dance, writing books and offering health consultation, as well as building my baby sling business in an effort to create personal empowerment and a solid financial base. Though my children were fatherless during those lean years, they were in the company of a mother who was striving for healthier relationships with men; they were observing the healing process of an emerging woman rather than enduring the hurtful cycle of a submissive mother. While my daughters were exposed to the rare dynamic of feminine self-care, my little son was learning to appreciate his feminine side and thus all women.

Finding time to nurture myself as well as my children is a juggling act which turns out to be easy simply because it is so necessary. When I take care of everybody else and neglect myself, everyone else eventually suffers. So I have learned how important it is to find moments here and there, even minutes and hours when family slumber rolls around, to recharge and remember all the inner work that awaits. Time management becomes a mother's best friend, as we balance out the many roles and responsibilities each day presents. As any mother well knows, random interruption is a component of the production process. Writing this book is a perfect example of what I am talking about. These last few paragraphs were interspersed with wiping a baby's bottom, cutting up oranges, nursing someone to sleep, putting away play-dough, and rewinding a children's tape.

When my third child Matthew was still an infant I kept a wide array of self-realization books on my writing table, strategically located next to my stuffed rocker where he would nurse, where my toddler would cuddle with me, and where my older daughter would sit on the arm of the chair while we home-schooled. When my lap wasn't filled with my offspring, it became a serving platter for all the inspirational books which healed me to the core, clawing away at what character traits were impeding both my personal growth and the quality of my mothering experience. I called it "Bittersweet Mothering" because of the combination of clearing the wreckage of my own past while assisting in the formation of a future generation, thus giving my children the primal mothering I never had.

Togetherness is the key factor. It is the cornerstone to the primal mothering experience. Trust and security are natural outgrowths of an unbroken bond. In today's society, where mother and child separation is the norm, mothers who obey their instincts and remain bonded to their babies are often looked upon as over-protective, martyristic, and downright neurotic. Courage and creativity become faithful companions to the mother who clings to her newborn, turns her back on social norm, and further relishes in the round-the-clock presence of her growing children.

People are always asking me how I can tolerate being around my children all the time. I have a hard time answering them because I don't understand the question. My instinct to remain connected to the primal needs of my children is as natural to me as drawing the next breath.

When I first began submitting articles to various magazines and making baby slings for the promotion of bonding, I was nurturing both my dream to be a writer and my determination to finance my family's needs minus the many-fold expenses of "going away" to a job. I was polishing my tin can, so to speak.

Though my housing came to an abrupt halt as a result of my choosing to live in our car over separating from my baby for the sake of earning rent money, I continued feeding the dream of writing and attaining financial independence while maintaining vigilance to family togetherness. Many of my eventually published stories were written by candlelight, late at night, as I sat in the back-seat of my old Chevy Impala while my toddler slept peacefully in the front. And by day I stopped every pregnant woman and mother/baby couple I saw, demonstrating the wonderful benefits of baby-wearing and selling slings along the way.

Some days were harder than others in those first years of mothering. When my only certainty resided in honoring my mothering instincts while all else in my life spelled confusion, I turned to Nature, the mother of us all for a vision quest of two to four days up on a mountain, alongside a river, or deep in the woods — just me, my daughter, a jug of water, and open ears which listened attentively to my inner voice. Sometimes I referred to spiritual recipes handed down by my favorite authors. Once, when confused about how to financially survive upon reaching my ultimate goal of moving to Hawaii, I performed one of my favorite exercises in self-discovery that I learned from the book **Illusions**. In this beautifully profound story of the reluctant Messiah, author Richard Bach wrote about turning any piece of literature into a magic book. He said, "You can do it with any book. You can do it with an old newspaper, if you read carefully enough. Haven't you done that, hold some problem in your mind, then open any book handy and see what it tells you?" I grabbed the closest book and let it fall open. With my eyes closed, I put my finger on a page and then, in search of meaning to my confusion, I proceeded to read the particular paragraph I was pointing to.

I could hardly believe my eyes! In this book about the spiritual journey of a powerful woman called Peace Pilgrim, she was using this exact paragraph to describe the time she went to

Hawaii and slept on the beaches of each island. She wrote about the beauty and peace of the people she met, and that safety from harm is a condition we create by virtue of our thoughts and expectations — whatever we think about expands. Reading this excerpt calmed my fears and further readied me for my upcoming journey.

Years before I heeded the call to become a mother, I had glimpses of the path which awaited me. In my twenties, while working as a burlesque dancer in the nightclubs of Seattle I was continually plagued by the question, "When I decide to be a mother someday, who will hold my baby while I'm on stage?" Obviously a smoky strip joint is no place for a baby, but the question in my mind back then made clear one important point: I was destined and determined to remain with my young when motherhood became my reality. My primal connection to mother-child togetherness was so potent that it out-shined the rules of society surrounding me.

And, years later, when mothering became a reality in my life, togetherness was simply a given. As a result of this instinctive conduct, my children and I have experienced homeless shelters, living in tents, living in and traveling in cars...but we've not chosen separation, so separation has not been our experience. Needless to say, we enjoy a rich volume of memories as a result of our choices. Like that Christmas Eve of 1991, in a two-person dome tent on the sands of a Hawaiian beach, homeschooling one child while pregnant with another.

I don't believe there is ever a time when we are denied the opportunity to live up to our mothering instincts. After all, the only thing that shatters dreams is compromise. We may have our imagination stretched beyond measure, but so are the rewards beyond measure — not only to ourselves and to our children, but to the generations ahead who represent the peaceful fruition of children raised according to the expectations of Nature.

If we hear ourselves saying, "I'd really like to be home with

my children but..." then maybe being home with our children
has lost its place on our list of priorities. I recall a friend crying
one evening while nursing her four-week old daughter. When I
asked what was wrong she sadly replied, "I have to wean my
baby because I need to go back to work in two weeks." Mind
you, this woman was a lactation consultant for the government
WIC program — an agency specifically designed to encourage
women to breastfeed! I assured her that other options existed
and enthusiastically offered alternatives until she curtly interrupted me by saying, "I have to go back to work because I love
fine clothes, expensive jewelry, and my new four-bedroom
house." When I suggested she take her daughter to work with
her, she quickly changed the subject.

Necessary trade-offs are a constant theme in the life of
women who choose primal mothering; shifting priorities from
possessing material things to instead having family togetherness, and mustering up the courage to traverse across lifestyles
unimaginable to the general public.

Courage is the mental or moral strength to venture, persevere,
and withstand danger, fear, or difficulty. What a gift, to show
our children that they win out over things which prove to be
ephemeral in the long run, like for instance making payments
on a new car.

One family I met had this credo — they refused to pay more
than three hundred dollars for a vehicle, and they did no auto
repairs on the cars they bought. When the car died, they simply
called the wrecking yard to tow it away, caught a cab home,
then proceeded to locate another vehicle for under three hundred dollars. As each car seemed to average a life-span of about
one year, they kept their yearly transportation costs far below
what they would have faced if hooked into the need for fancier
transportation.

The irony I have had the pleasure of knowing is the fact that,
with my cornerstone of family togetherness firmly in place, all
of my personal desires still come to fruition. With conviction

and creativity, I have managed to finish my college education with my first-born in a baby sling, give lectures to large audiences with a toddler playing at my feet, and run a home business writing books and making baby slings while homeschooling three children.

It's easier to play the role of a victim and have excuses for why we can't do what we want than it is to accept responsibility for turning our wishes into reality. In the words of James Allen, "The greatest achievement was at first and for a time a dream. The oak sleeps in the acorn; the bird waits in the egg; and in the highest vision of the soul a waking angel stirs. Dreams are the seedlings of realities." We are mothers with a mission, but we are also people with a purpose. My book **Anatomy Of An Accomplishment** is designed to help us remember our underlying purpose on the planet, that we may become fully functioning artists in our own lives. As females, our nurturing skills go beyond the immediate mothering experience. The fate of humanity depends on the female intellect in all of its capacities.

Feeding our talents while fueling the future generation is a balancing act which leaves us feeling elated and soul-satisfied. Women have been expected to make a choice rather than nurture both their children and their calling. The truth of the matter is our world needs the impact of female intelligence just as much as our children need primal mothering throughout a given day. Joseph Chilton Pearce proclaims, "God knows we need women in our politics and our medical places. We need some of that base intelligence there in every walk of life." Women belong wherever they want to be, in whatever capacity they can best serve humanity, and children have a right to be with mom.

We need to take back our babies, our lives, our minds, and our bodies. The medical establishment has built a financial empire by relying heavily on their female clients. And somehow we have come to depend soley on these "experts" for such natural practices as pregnancy, birthing, and caring for our young. An even sadder thing about this displacement of power is that some women have put so much of their faith in the medical establishment they actually dissuade other females from taking back their primal power. I remember the deluge of unsupportive mail I received from readers of a particular newsletter I wrote for, after the publication of my story about choosing an unassisted birth after my previous C-section. The editor of the periodical had ended my article with a plea to her readers to discourage me from my "irresponsible" decision to birth alone.

There are plenty of people who find it their duty to keep us obedient to social limitation, but nothing can stop the woman who has glimpsed her power as a primal mother. Those of us who feel this rebellion towards modern mothering practices lay rationalization theory aside and increase the volume on our intuition. We are not swaying to the latest convenient theory about child development, but rather, we are happily humming to the tune of our own heart.

A Native American philosophy reminds us that in all deliberations we must consider the impact our decisions will make on the seventh generation from now. Primal mothering is earth-friendly; an environmentally-sound lifestyle which respects our bodies, the bodies of our children, the body of Mother Earth, and the psyche of all involved. Those of us who follow our mothering instincts literally grow up inside ourselves, imparting that primal wisdom and personal strength to our daughters while ensuring our sons a safe home called Earth where violence is unacceptable. In turn, our daughters will find it quite natural to take responsibility for their mothering choices rather than let society dictate rules which don't reflect the true needs of their young. By the seventh generation, primal mothering, the natural way to raise humanity, will become normal and prevalent.

This book will change the course of humanity by bringing mothers and their offspring back into daily harmony. Women looking within, transforming within and then, by collective effort, transforming our species. This book is for all women, single or with partner, because the true, primal needs of our children remain the same regardless of our marital status. Mothering is about Nature, having nothing to do with our intimate attachments. Once that egg is fertilized we are mothers first. Our deepest attachment becomes that undying, ever-present role in the lives of dependent children — the seedlings of humanity who rely on us at every turn.

Does all this sound idealistic? Does it seem impossible for the efforts of one primal mother to make a difference? Keep in mind the Hundredth Monkey concept, wherein one monkey choosing to wash her sweet potato at the river's edge caused a shift in the consciousness of monkeys on other shores. When enough people think and act a certain way, a shift in social consciousness inevitably takes place, and that's exactly what I'm advocating for the betterment of humanity. We need to roll up our sleeves and begin washing sweet potatoes at the river's edge; we need to honor the call of primal mothering because such obedience to our instincts satisfies our hormones and nurtures the heart of future generations.

Think about this...less than a generation ago, NO SMOKING sections were basically non-existent. And handicap access was seldom a concern of the architect. Today, because enough people (and really not that many) rolled up their sleeves and started washing sweet potatoes — so to speak — smoke-free environments are now the norm, and an architect wouldn't think of investing time in a blueprint which did not include the needs of a physically-challenged minority.

When we decide to trust the flow that flourishes as a result of our heart-felt convictions we are assured of the coincidences which guide us on our journey. We tap into a universal language that speaks to our hearts rather than hearing social moors that speak to our fears. And the primal link between mothers across all cultures becomes clear to us as we work together in defense of today's children and tomorrow's generations.

We are strong mothers building a gentle world. When we learn to respond to our primal mothering instincts instead of reacting to social pressure we come into our personal strength. In **Tao Of Motherhood** Vimala McClure writes, "The truly feminine mother never cringes or defers. Her strength is unshakable, like the earth upon which we walk but which can topple us with a single deep breath."

This is the generation of women taking all the time they need to heal themselves while learning to meet the needs of their young; giving children all they need to grow into humans having a life experience which doesn't require healing in the first place. Commitment is the key that turns conviction into reality. This book is my commitment to add to the literary ranks an owner's manual for those of us who occupy the feminine vehicle andwho accept the responsibility of raising humanity.

Chapter 2

PREGNANCY
Building The Baby Within

"It may be that the first stage in an effective global revolution for peace will be when male doctors accept progressively to retire from obstetrics and return childbirth to women."
— **Michel Odent, MD**

When our female vehicle is activated into the developing role of motherhood, we are hormonally and psychically equipped for the journey. There is nothing lacking. We only need to listen closely to our inner voice and then courageously live up to what that voice is saying. A male-dominated mentality with all its medical gadgetry has driven most of us women out of hearing distance of our instincts, but the primal hormones keep coursing through us, ever-reminding we are equipped with the tools to birth humanity anew.

While stretching my body at the beach one day, a physically-fit man approached me and asked, "Where did you get your yoga training?" I had to laugh. I've never taken a yoga class in my life. I was simply following my body's request for movement as I reconnected to childhood memories and my body's ability to resemble the likes of Gumby — capable of moving every which way and loose. The man seemed perplexed because, after years of study, he had not accomplished some of the stretching poses which came naturally to me.

And so it is with pregnancy. While the experts argue amongst themselves and espouse varied viewpoints enough to confuse any information-seeker, the majority of females around the world (human and non-human alike) go silently along from conception to birth with not a complication considered or created.

Without experts tarnishing our instincts, the primal woman in each of us can heed the inner call and simply manage to do right, from start to finish. We all possess this primal instinct, and it is my goal to help you clear away the mental debris that may be separating you from this internal knowledge and wisdom which has successfully carried humanity through its entirety.

It is only the last few centuries of "expertise" which have oppressed our intuition. With such a long and impressive record of primal success resting beneath technology's top layer of intrusion, it won't take too much effort to unearth the shine of primal mothering.

Part of the responsibility of mothering is recognizing when we are truly ready for the responsibility of mothering. Upon learning that we are pregnant, the first thing we need to ask ourselves is "Do I want to be pregnant?" Not every woman thrills at the sight of a urine-stick turned YES. For whatever reason, whether we are a teen-ager who doesn't feel ready, a woman who prefers to wait, or a mother who already feels overwhelmed, we must be honest with ourselves. I, personally, have had several opportunities to practice this rigorous form of self-honesty.

As a child, I once had a dream that showed me giving birth to my first child when I turned thirty-two, after receiving a college degree in Philosophy. The message in that dream stayed with me to serve as a time-line and psychological guide for the upcoming years of turbulence.

My twenties were defined by drug addiction, eating disorders, sexual promiscuity, and every other fatal bonding attempt known to the insecure mind. That decade of confusion was accompanied by several pregnancies, all of which ended in spontaneous miscarriage or abortion. Then, shortly before my 32nd birthday and in my senior year of collegiate study, six months after I had become sober and somewhat secure within myself, I became pregnant again. With the baby's due date one month after graduation, I knew the time had come for me to step into the reality of my childhood dream.

Most women I knew had begun their mothering careers at a younger age, and there were plenty of people who expressed concern that I might face complications as a result of being in my thirties. I started connecting with other women who were still enjoying pregnancies right into their forties, and quickly overcame all concern over the timing of my pregnancy.

Today I have three children. During each of these pregnancies I used the gestation period as a time for major re-construction of my life so as to create a future which would accommodate my personal and financial needs while staying true to mother and child togetherness. I did the best I could with my outer world, knowing full well my success in that arena would pale in comparison to the joy of non-negotiable togetherness. I kept in mind the words of Thic Nhat Nanh from the book **For A Future To Be Possible**, "The wealthy are often the least able to make others happy. Only those with time can do so."

My first-born Sarah Lee was conceived after several months of psychic interaction. She often came to me in dreams, always saying the same thing..."Get your act together, I'm on my way." An important message indeed, for at the time I was heavily addicted to drugs and my personal life was a mess. Her insistent words jolted me into action and, by the time I became pregnant, I had six months of sobriety from drugs, lived in a nice apartment, and made enough money from my job to begin saving.

This conception pulled together all the pieces. Though I had earlier dropped out of college to follow my urge to experience Mexico where I was permanently altered by the sight of that breastfeeding mother I referred to in chapter one, I was just one semester away from completing my undergraduate degree. I would be thirty-two years old before my baby was born, and my last abortion was accompanied by a dream telling me that my next pregnancy marked the beginning of my mothering career.

Upon learning of this pregnancy my instincts took over and I knew that city life, the high cost of living, and the stress therein were not conducive to the needs of my developing family.

I, along with my then-husband, packed up our little red Vega station-wagon and bought a small dome tent on our way out of Oklahoma City. We located a small college town along a beautiful river where our new "home" was pitched. I enrolled at the university and found work at a nearby convenience store.

Thinking ahead to what would be the most efficient and economical lifestyle for raising my baby, I decided to earn the money for a small 20-foot travel-home and rent a lot at the trailer park located just across the street from the university. The affordable, cozy, and convenient living situation along with expanding education goals gave me a wonderful sense of comfort, and the cornerstone — my commitment to the career of mothering — held steady. Thoughts of continuing on to graduate school offered not only a strengthening of my education but also an opportunity to receive student loans which would keep my family financially afloat.

With my second pregnancy, my dream of moving to Hawaii was being nurtured. Once again, prior to conception I received nocturnal visits from this coming child. She strongly stated, "My name is Jasmine and, if you will let me come through, I promise that we will all be on an airplane headed for Hawaii by the day you are three months pregnant."

Now I had not even been considering the idea of having another child. But I had been obsessed with the intense desire to raise Sarah Lee in Hawaii. At the time of Jasmine's message I was without the financial means to change my living situation. We were merely living from hand to mouth. It seemed inconceivable that a move to Hawaii could materialize. Jasmine's message returned one day as I was swimming in a cold creek, trying to convince myself that Hawaii wasn't that important to me. With a faded half moon hovering overhead, I surrendered to Jasmine's encouraging push forward and that night I became pregnant.

True to the metaphysical law that the universe conspires to help those who follow their dreams, my baby sling business suddenly blossomed into a deluge of mail-orders, a friend whose son worked for the airlines got us a huge discount on two one-way tickets and, despite all my disbelief, we were on a Hawaii-bound airplane the day I turned three month's pregnant! Me, Sarah Lee, and in-utero Jasmine Kokee landed on the island of Kauai with $84.00 in my purse and a housing invitation that would expire in three short weeks.

We bought a small dome tent (I knew I should have kept the one from my first pregnancy!) and hitch-hiked to a beautiful beach on the dry side of the island where I set up house and lived happily throughout the next six months of my pregnancy.

My third pregnancy was equally motivating. This time, I was sure I wasn't having any more children. Then came the message..."My name is Matthew and my gift to you is peace." At the time of this celestial whisper, inner peace was sorely lacking in my life. Though I was straight-up with my mission of mothering, my personal purpose was getting off-track. I had specifically moved to Hawaii to raise my children in a warm environment where fruit grew abundantly AND to write motivational health books amidst the inspiring beauty of this tropical Paradise.

I was presently off-course, hiring myself out as a writer rather than heeding the inner call of so many projects residing in my soul. When I'm not living up to the definition of my dreams I'm stuck with a grinding anxiety that keeps inner peace at bay.

Matthew was challenging me to expand my mothering responsibilities which, in turn, turned up the desire on getting my financial/career act together.

Could I handle three children by myself? How was peace going to materialize in a situation which appeared to me to be potentially overwhelming? Then I remembered those days of homelessness that gave way to healthier choices with the coming of Sarah Lee, as well as my skepticism when Jasmine promised Hawaii. In both cases, it all worked out — once I committed to the journey.

This third pregnancy saw my writing career blossoming. Book after book resided in my soul, waiting to be brought forth in the written form. Matthew was demanding attention to my writing goals as well as to my financial future. After all, writing books would not be just about feeding my purpose but it would also feed my family.

I wanted to set the scene for raising three children and writing books. I created our dream home — a quaint cottage with a huge yard and a sweeping view of the ocean — where I could comfortably grow the baby within and watch my girls play while tending to my writing career.

One of the myths about pregnancy I find rather ironic is the idea we are now in a weakened state and need to "take it easy." Nothing could be further from the truth. Pregnancy is a time when my life seems to be at full throttle emotionally, psychically, mentally, spiritually, and physically. With my first child, at six months pregnant I was working as a stocker in a grocery store in the afternoons and on weekends, wrapping burritos at the local fast-food place every night, attending college full-time, swimming thirty minutes daily, and dancing up a storm at pow wows on weekends. With my second child, I was walking as much as ten miles each day, foraging for fruit, hiking, and dancing every night on the sandy beaches of Hawaii. With my third child, I also walked several miles daily but with the added weight of two-year-old Jasmine on my back.

Sessions of exercise, especially the art of dance, gave me a chance to more intimately interact with my womb-babies. Though I had been an exotic dancer for ten years prior to mothering, and studied ballet at length during college, none of my training compared to the internship which accompanied my prenatal experiences. With each of my three pregnancies a specific dance style — along with particular preferences in music — proved to reflect the unique personalities of each of my emerging children.

My first daughter Sarah Lee is a powerfully psychic and extremely compassionate child whose visionary skills are beyond measure. From the moment of conception I found myself swaying to songs like "That's The Way Of The World" by Earth, Wind, & Fire and "Imagine" by John Lennon. As the pregnancy progressed, those songs took a back-seat to Indian drumming, and I was at every pow wow within a fifty-mile radius, dancing solid until midnight. Just hours before giving birth I was twirling and rocking to the ancient beat of the drum.

My second daughter Jasmine Kokee is capable of intriguing and teaching everyone around her, strangers and family members alike. She transcends all boundaries. How profound, that the songs I felt compelled to embrace throughout her womb-time included such feminist classics as "I Am Woman" and "You And Me Against The World." Jasmine insisted I dance several hours each night of her in-utero development. In my ninth month, when I felt too tired to participate in late-night dance vigils, my arms started itching terribly and I heard this faint voice telling me that only dancing would make the itching go away. It worked! As most of my pregnancy was spent living out of a tent along the splendid beaches of Hawaii, I met with my tape player each night, just outside my blue cloth dome-home where I watched the water splash seductively over the reef as my blossoming belly took over, tiredness fading away.

My youngest, Matthew Renee is an observing soul who, though fully aware of his rights and willing to defend them at every turn, assumes a relaxed and peaceful personality. His womb-time was accompanied by popular love songs and, to my complete surprise, country & western music! Each night from my bay window I would look out at the Pacific ocean and feel a depth of inner peace unbeknownst to me in pregnancies prior. Cher's beautiful song "After All" became a favorite, followed closely by "Wind Beneath My Wings." In the air was an element of romance, a developing love for myself, and the prompt deliverance of a peace promised in those moments after conception.

This three-fold experience with meeting my children more deeply through the art of dance and song paved the way for me to meet myself more deeply in the same way. Even now, in this postpartum world of mine, each night finds me slipping away from the family bed where my three angels sleep, donning a soft pink nightgown, easing state-of-the-art earphones over my thickly braided hair, and tuning in to the oldies but goodies that nurture my soul and make me grow.

Exercise serves many purposes in pregnancy, one of which is preparing our bodies for birth itself. However, those of us in the best of physical shape can still end up with compromising birth experiences.

The single most important area of personal responsibility during pregnancy lies in revealing to ourselves any and all belief systems about birth, and clearing away any emotional issues which may stand in our way of enjoying a perfect pregnancy and a blissful birth. Understanding past birth experiences as well as the cultural messages we have received up to this point makes it easier to correct areas which might otherwise impede our path as we approach the birth of our child.

Birth-clearing exercises are an excellent tool for transforming our psyche so that we become more in tune with our primality. One of my favorite exercises is called "The Great Debate." In the book **I Could Do Anything** author Barbara Sher writes, "Whenever you leave your tribe (think differently than the social norm) or even consider leaving your tribe, you set off a debate in your mind between two skilled and ruthless teams of debaters, each of which claims to represent you. Make those debaters in your head go on record. Their arguments contain important information for you, and you need to get it onto paper where you can take a good look at it. Divide a sheet of paper into two columns. In one column record assertions of the personal voice, so label this 'Personal.' The other column is for the voices of conformity, the tribal voice, and should be labeled 'Tribal.' As you do this exercise and learn from it, your tribal voice will not suddenly disappear. It will keep disapproving, but from now on you will stop confusing it with your own intuition."

Here's the exercise I did when pregnant with Matthew:

I want to birth alone, in the privacy of my home:

Tribal: What if something goes wrong? You'll hate yourself forever.

Personal: Learning to trust myself and believe in my heart-felt desires is so important to me that I am willing to take any risks necessary to complete my dream of primal mothering. I've denied myself a totally sovereign birth twice. I'm taking everything I learned into this present experience. I am ready and prepared for this.

Tribal: But what if the cord is wrapped around the baby's neck?

Personal: Then I'll unwrap it. I'm not willing to dwell on what can go wrong when just as much energy can be used to instigate, and thus manifest, a positive outcome.

Tribal: You should have somebody there. It's irresponsible to jeopardize the life of you or your baby. And who's going to cut the cord?

Personal: Cutting an umbilical cord is not an academic endeavor. My responsibility is to listen to myself and vote on faith, not make decisions out of fear. Your fear-based perception is not my reality. Keep it to yourself, thank you.

If we can anticipate problems, then we can prevent them. And our biggest problem, notoriously, is our own mentality. I highly recommend Jane Roberts' book **The Nature Of Personal Reality** for the purpose of separating yourself from any debilitating beliefs that could potentially pull you down at a time when you are designed to be experiencing life's all-time high: Pregnancy and Birth.

The clearing of our physical environment is a confirmation of our personal inner growth. By my third pregnancy I was becoming an expert hound at smelling out all the stress factors in daily life, and reducing tension where I could. Traffic jams and child-detested car seats led me to the decision to sell my car. I started a savings account with the money and moved to a house within walking distance of everything I needed. I reduced the stress of driving and instigated an excellent exercise program. With Jasmine in the backpack and my expanding belly of Matthew Renee, Sarah Lee roller-skated in front of me as I pulled the shopping cart into town for our daily supply of fruit from the market and books from the library, smelling roses along the way instead of fighting off exhaust fumes in traffic.

I revamped my priorities and prepared for the lifestyle which awaited me — raising three children. Hurricane Iniki had taught me a valuable lesson about the truth of necessities. The massive storm had taken away electricity and telephone service for several months. By candle-light I changed diapers and came in touch with need versus convenience.

I used that previously-attained knowledge to whittle my

financial world down to need, as I felt driven by my intuition to develop a substantial savings account by the time of Matthew's birth. It seemed so odd to be a welfare mother living below the poverty level and yet devising a plan to save as much as $1,000 in the months to come. I put a 100% commitment behind that goal.

An unexpected stress caught me quite by surprise when, in my sixth month of pregnancy I began feeling irritable toward nursing my toddler. My nipples were becoming increasingly sensitive and I finally — though reluctantly — made the choice to stop nursing Jasmine who was then almost three, until after her brother's birth. Some mothers breeze all the way through their pregnancies with no nipple discomfort while others, like myself, develop intolerant levels of nipple sensitivity and prefer taking temporary weaning measures rather than nursing a resentment toward their offspring.

You can count on people — peers and professionals alike — telling you it's harmful to be nursing while pregnant, that your older child is taking away valuable nutrients from both you and your growing fetus. Just tell them it's your legitimate excuse for eating as much as you want! After all, an uptake in nutritional output justifies increased nutritional input. In other words, it all balances out.

Speaking of eating as much as you want...make sure those food choices are serving your highest nutritional needs as well as the developing needs of your womb-baby. When I am pregnant I feel naturally inclined to increase the nuts, seeds, avocados, and leafy greens in my fruitarian diet.

Choices other than delectable fruits, vegetables, nuts, and seeds have the propensity to create unwanted weight. How many times have you heard an overweight woman admit she never lost those pounds after her first baby was born? I hear it all the time, and it's a misery which can be avoided. When I ran my baby sling business, I spoke daily with women who expressed their frustration at having gained too much weight

during their pregnancies. They also conveyed a sense of futility for never being able to take the weight off in pregnancies
prior.

I'll save discussions on natural nutrition for a later chapter
because what I'm mostly concerned with here is the self-esteem
that suffers as a result of unnecessary weight-gain during pregnancy. When that baby finally slithers blissfully from your
beautiful body, nothing is more satisfying than being excited at
the prompt return of your pre-pregnant state. It's like lending
something special to a close friend; it's a pleasure to have it
returned to you in as good or better condition than when you
first handed it over.

Having babies doesn't have to ruin our body. Creating another human being requires about twenty pounds to accommodate
baby, placenta, amniotic fluid and breast enlargement. Do yourself a favor. Include high self-esteem with your pregnancy and
birthing plans. When you gently release your precious child
somewhere between hanging laundry and preparing dinner, be
able to soon thereafter reach into your closet and take out that
favorite outfit you've had on hold since you were about five
months pregnant. Practice the dietary principles necessary to
feel great about yourself after the birth, when your newborn is
nursing peacefully at your breast while you enjoy meals without feeling frustrated, defeated, or obese.

There are so many delightful fruits, vegetables, nuts, and
seeds which don't add unnecessary weight. Though I sometimes succumbed to cooked-food cravings during my pregnancies, I basically focused on eating what my body needed most
— fresh, raw, natural, unadulterated foods. I remember how
happy I felt just ten hours after giving birth, walking my three
children up to the health-food store and feeling slim and trim in
a silky skirt that had been patiently awaiting my pre-pregnant
state. I rewarded myself with the purchase of several fresh
organic figs which, at $8.00 per pound, proved to also be a

reward for having reached my financial goal of $1,000 before the birth of Matthew!

Feeling pretty is important. Pregnancy leads us through constant physical expansion and, in a society where flat stomachs are worshipped, the pregnant woman needs to generate her own sense of beauty. Most maternity clothes are designed to cover up our big-ness. In pregnancy, I choose to counteract this closet mentality by gently wrapping my blossoming womanhood with beautiful pareos... a Polynesian skirt/dress that ties at the waist or around the neck. From conception to birth and beyond, my loyal pareo meets my wardrobe needs. Skirts, such as a pareo, are especially comfortable because I don't experience the confinement which accompanies maternity pants. And, in those last months of pregnancy when I spend so much time going to the bathroom to relieve my cramped bladder, it's much easier to lift a loose skirt than to peel slacks over my huge baby-belly.

It's so much fun to buy baby clothes and get ready for our blossoming bundle of joy. My infant clothing package includes several flannel receiving blankets, three to four dozen cloth diapers, plenty of diaper covers and diaper pins, two or more cotton baby slings, and several nightgowns that snap all the way down. I absolutely hate trying to dress a newborn in anything which has to go over their head. I figure they already paid their dues by pressing through such a narrow channel between the womb and the world. The least I can do is make dressing-time more comfortable. For the most part, my newborns enjoy the freedom of nudity. Occasional cool weather and the pleasure of dry bedding at night are my motivators for having the right infant wardrobe on hand.

For those who choose to use diapers, cloth is best for a variety of reasons, the first being that cotton feels better against the skin than plastic. What would you think about trading in your designer cotton-wear and spending the next two years of your life encased in bulky plastic panties?

The next reason has to do with health. Babies who wear disposable plastic diapers are notorious for experiencing diaper rash, and few things are more painful for a baby than a sore and stinging bottom. There are many chemicals in plastic diapers that, when combined with the acidity of our baby's urine, create a fertile environment for bacteria. The next reason has to do with finances. When you buy three dozen cloth diapers and some diaper covers, your initial financial outlay becomes the end of consumerism on this subject.

For their entire infancy and beyond, your baby's diapering needs are met; as will be the needs of their potential younger sibling who has yet to be conceived or considered. On the contrary, with disposable plastic diapers you are making regular trips to the store, laying down money which could be better spent on anything but some product that is compromising in comfort, unhealthy to our babies, and a menace to the planet.

And then there's the more primal approach that, for the most part, eliminates the need for diapers. It's called elimination timing. Have you ever wondered how women throughout the ages dealt with motherhood minus diapers? Mothers can actually learn to respond to the cues of their young. Babies produce a little sound and/or body signal right before they eliminate. By holding our infants over a receptacle, they can actually develop an understanding of communicating their elimination needs to us. We simply hold our babies, resting their heads against our chest and their backs against our stomachs while holding their little legs under the thighs to make a squat posture. Also, by using a sound like "psss" or "sshh" when we hold our babies out, an effective pattern of communication gets established. At night, rather than putting diapers on our babies, we can have a plastic pad covered with thick cotton underneath them in the event we don't wake up to hear their subtle evening cues. Otherwise, we can keep a receptacle by the bed and simply place them in the squat position, then return to a warm and dry embrace in the family bed.

Most mothers feel perplexed about building a baby's

wardrobe prior to birth because they don't know whether their baby is a girl or a boy. Baby girls are given the joy of a rainbow while boys are relegated to blue. Pretty dresses by-pass the infant male experience altogether. This is just another example of how women allow society to dictate their decisions without even questioning. Homophobia is often at the root of this infant clothing paranoia, yet the fearing public doesn't take into consideration the fact that our male homosexual population was once a generation of baby boys who were assigned blue, and denied the pleasures of prettiness. A primal mother doesn't make her decisions based on the fear-based opinions of society.

My three-year-old son Matthew has a wardrobe which consists of shorts, shirts, skirts, and dresses...loose-fitting soft cotton and flannel dresses. He loves spinning around and feeling the fabric sway against his legs. Just the other day a man originally from the Orient asked me why I let my son wear dresses. I explained to him that I don't believe in sex discrimination of any sort, including the choice of clothing, and further reminded him that most cultures, even America right up to the time of the founding fathers, have readily accepted the idea of men in clothing that is free about the legs. He quickly admitted to me that, had his mother let him wear dresses and skirts when he was a little boy, he too, would be wearing one right now. His testimony was accompanied by a certain sadness and sense of loss. Little boys who are denied personal expression, whether it's about clothes in general or colors in particular, are missing out on the joys of a versatile wardrobe and a wide range of emotional feelings.

Since our feet are servant to both traveler and passenger, they deserve the best we can offer them during this journey known as pregnancy. I've always adhered to the barefoot approach to motherhood, but for those who prefer a bit of distance between the soles of their feet and the soil of the earth, I highly recommend shoes which cater to the natural form of your foot.

Obviously raised heels don't fit into the scheme of natural footwear.

Through all three of my pregnancies, I have not developed stretch marks which I believe is due to the fact I rubbed my belly, thighs, and bottom with olive oil each day. This daily discipline felt wonderful as I took time out to nurture myself and massage my in-resident child.

Common sense suggests that drugs have no place in pregnancy. However, if we are actively involved in the use of alcohol or other drugs the insidious nature of drug dependency can blur our decision-making. Thus, it is helpful to participate in a support group for the sake of abstaining from that which will harm both ourselves and our babies. I have always relied on twelve-step programs such as Alcoholics Anonymous to master any particular habit which doesn't belong in my life in general and my pregnancy in particular.

During a rebirthing session (a technique developed by Leonard Orr whereby you lie down, breathe in deeply and rapidly for an hour or longer to release stress and trauma held in the tissues of the body), I recalled/relived my feelings about life inside my mother's womb. My memories were primarily centered around the anxiety I felt as a result of the constant flood of nicotine and caffeine which was coming through my mother's bloodstream. Just keep in mind we share virtually everything with our baby; our food, our cigarettes, our alcohol, even our emotions.

Speaking of emotions, given the fact it takes two to tango, pregnancy inevitably brings with it the need to deal with, heal from, let go of, or further commit to a relationship with our unborn baby's father. If you are in a healthy relationship and both of you look forward to the shared commitment of parenting, that's great. Keep doing what works, and keep enjoying the fruits of your efforts. But not all of us experience companionship after conception. People break up. Abandonment by a partner upon learning of a pregnancy is common, and men abusing women during pregnancy is devastatingly real.

My partner at the time of Sarah Lee's conception was a practicing alcoholic who was both verbally and physically abusive. My mothering instincts quickly taught me that pregnancy is a time of not putting up with any shit! By my sixth month of pregnancy, the she-bear within had grown to the point that I counter-attacked his abuse with a blow so substantial he never once laid a hand on me again. Though the physical violence had stopped, the alcohol drinking and verbal digs continued to the point that I gained enough self-esteem to demand a better world for myself and my child.

No matter how you slice it, the bottom line is that WE are the ones who are pregnant, WE are ultimately responsible for the act of baby-building, and WE are fast approaching the all-consuming role of mother. Pregnancy is a one-woman show, oftentimes accompanied by caring partners, but just as often staged without a crew. Nature has designed us to be autonomous in matters concerning pregnancy, birth, and raising humanity. We have what it takes to satisfy the requirements of raising our young, with or without a partner.

Those seemingly unplanned pregnancies can be the toughest, when we subconsciously rely on this turn of events to overcome any problems existing inside an intimate relationship. I call this "romancing the zygote." Under these circumstances we need to really face ourselves and be sure the continuation of our pregnancy is not fueled chiefly by the assumption that "he'll change his mind and want to marry me" or "he'll quit drinking and become a responsible father," or whatever it is that we wish would change as a result of having "his" baby. The fate of my last pregnancy was a hard one to decide upon because my relationship to the father had sadly ended a month before I knew I was pregnant. I was scared at the prospect of being a mother to three children, yet at the same time I serenely accepted the challenge which lay before me until the day I learned Matthew's father and his extended family wanted nothing to do with this coming child. My emotional entanglement with Matthew's father left me torn between continuing with the pregnancy and having the abortion I assumed would please this man. It took a great deal of soul-searching to break free from this codependency, to decide for myself what was to be.

This dilemma goes both ways. If we need to postpone the call of motherhood and the father disagrees, so be it. Nothing is more important to our mental health than to be honest with ourselves and take action necessary to nurture that honesty. The argument is not about being pro-life or pro-choice; it's about being pro-woman that she may have control over her life. I've been on both sides of this fence, and each time I needed to muster up the self-love necessary to make such a heartfelt decision. Believe me, if men became pregnant, abortion would be a sacrament.

For the sake of your own serenity, your child's self-esteem, and the birth experience itself, I encourage you to work through any resentments and expectations you may have regarding your relationship to the biological father of your child. Codependency recovery is a valuable tool for dealing with this issue. It's also very important to look at inner-child healing as an avenue for working through relationship issues, since our intimate relationships tend to mirror the core relationships we had while growing up.

It's all inter-related. I have come to recognize the correlation between my attraction to emotionally unavailable men and having been raised by a father who simply could not express any emotion except rage. Thus, my adulthood has been plagued with relationships wherein I feel unloved and afraid. It is for this very reason that my children are from three different fathers. It took years of self-discovery work to find the core of my attractions so I could finally change my life-script. Motherhood called long before my ability to manifest and maintain a healthy intimate relationship. Today, I enjoy the nurturing qualities of healthy male friendships because I dove deep to find the roots of my fatal attractions, then nurtured my way home to being treated with respect.

Society treats pregnancy as a disease while accepting the status quo of unsatisfactory relationships. What if, instead of going to doctors to treat our pregnancies, we went to support groups and therapists specializing in women's issues to treat our feelings and heal our relationships during the course of a perfectly primal, self-governing, truly pleasant pregnancy?

Another homework assignment designed to be completed in the course of our pregnancies is addressing the subject of birth itself. Society has molded a belief system about birth to be one of fear, pain, complications, and necessary medical direction. So many women are told their baby is too big, their pelvic region is too small, or any other number of diagnoses which lead medical experts to automatically and authoritatively plug into "barbaric" birthing practices. Let us not forget obstetrics is the second highest paid profession, just behind surgeons, which could explain why obstetricians are steadily increasing their practice of performing C-sections.

Let us also not forget the miraculous wonders of a naturally expanding pelvis during birth, when we are relaxed and in harmony with our body and our baby, when the physical environment and people therein are comforting rather than condescending. Since the reality of our birth experience is merely a reflection of earlier actions (or inactions) taken, we need to delve deep so as to create the birth of our desires.

Emotional clearing during these months of blossoming motherhood takes us on a myriad of disclosures, as we call a spade a spade and awaken to our sovereignty. It's a time when we need to look within for our answers and overcome the urge to hand our power over to others. I went so far as to have my telephone service disconnected in my last pregnancy because well-meaning friends were aghast at my self-governing approach to pregnancy and birth, and my confidence was wavering in light of this barrage of disapproval. Too many times I had reached out through "Ma Bell" for my answers instead of getting quiet enough to hear my intuition speak, soft and true. I pitted my sovereignty against social chatter and developed the courage to argue for my convictions.

In many ways, pregnancy was a lonely time. I ached for the circle of loving support that humanity once knew. I longed for the sisterhood of women who in times past were deeply rooted in their power, for the brotherhood who expressed awe and respect for the natural abilities of their sisters. I humbly accepted the reality that my Purpose in this life was to carry the message of primal mothering. It was my task, sometimes a lonely journey often accompanied by persecution, to reconnect women to their Primal Power, and to restore humanity to that loving support. Somehow, knowing the magnitude of my mission, the lonesome feelings slipped away to be replaced by awesome gratitude. Like Jonathan Livingston Seagull who flew away beyond the far cliffs of social consciousness, my sadness was not so much about solitude as it was that others refused to recognize the joyful healing found in primal mothering. And anyway, I wasn't really alone; I had the sacred company of my womb-baby.

I learned to speak to my baby. Prenatal psychology being the latest breakthrough in the field of human development, I was enjoying regular and consistent communication with my unborn as proof of what research now suggests. Before going to sleep at night, I talked to my babies. I asked questions about their in-utero needs; was I eating sufficiently for their optimum growth? What did they prefer in the way of my exercise program? What were their hopes and fears about the upcoming birth? I also shared with them all my fears and joys, expectations, and such. I often awoke in the morning to their messages sweetly implanted on my psyche. I relied on this avenue of communications for questions as important as whether they were in a good position to be born and what position I should assume at the exact time of birth. In one dream, in-utero Matthew showed me he would be turning head-down during labor, so for me not to worry about whether his head was engaged prior to that, and in another dream I was on all fours in my living room at the time of his birth, with little Sarah Lee supporting his head as he descended from my body.

By the way, just because "head-down" is the most popular position at the time of birth does not mean any variations from this theme are wrong. The birthing knowledge contained between a woman and her child is sufficient to bring about the end result.

I think the most burning question in my mind with each of my pregnancies was, what position will I end up giving birth in? I wanted to be physically fit for all possible options. Gardening proved to be an excellent all-around preparation for birth. The squatting position was especially helpful for opening my pelvic region. I watch little children as they naturally assume the primal position of squatting, and find my intuition reminding me of the fact that squatting during childbirth is the most natural and common position for primal mothers.

With all this preparation work — clearing the past and planning for the future — living in the present can seem to elude us. That's where practices like meditation and yoga come into play. It's also a good idea to bathe ourselves in spiritually nourishing literature and tapes which keep us aware of our moment-by-moment world. One book which has really helped me is **The Precious Present** by Spencer Johnson. It's a beautifully simple story which takes less than an hour to read. I made a point of reading it every day of my pregnancies.

Preparation for birth begins with conception because there is so much we need to unlearn. Unlike what we have been taught, birth is not just about proper breathing techniques or when to push. In fact, as you will learn in the next chapter, we needn't "breathe" correctly nor "push" our babies out. We do, however, need to know ourselves well enough to allow our instincts the opportunity to orchestrate birth as it was intended by Nature.

Every woman deserves the sense of accomplishment derived from shedding authority and embracing her own sovereignty. By withdrawing our energies from the medical establishment and building a strong foundation in Self, we in effect become students of our higher knowing and surrender to the Truth of Creation.

If the upcoming birth experience is not our first, then we can look at our previous birth(s) and awaken to the dynamics which were involved. What didn't we like? What appeared to go wrong? Where did we go against our intuition? What could we have done differently?

Rewrite those births to reflect the way we really wanted them to go. Then create affirmations to support that vision and tape them up everywhere! Make book-marks depicting their messages. Some of my birth affirmations included:

I enjoy a sense of grace during birth.

I show absolutely no signs of fear or concern.

My only responsibility is to control my mind; my body will birth my baby safely and efficiently.

Just courage and patience are required to send my baby merrily into my loving arms.

I see birth as a personal challenge, and I am confident I am up to the task.

I give birth in safety and solitude.

As long as I am alone and able to yield to the sexual joy of the birthing, I am able to experience wonderful orgasmic feelings and no pain at all. I believe my baby's birth will come quickly, quietly, and easily.

I keep my legs, arms, face and pelvic floor completely relaxed.

I believe steadfastly in what I see in the hours of vision and clear sky.

Inundate yourself with positive feelings about birth and take time every day to visualize this coming birth EXACTLY as you want it to be. Though the details of the visualization may change from day to day, it's the essence of the experience which really matters — how you'll feel inside the experience. Make best friends with my book **I Can Do This! An Unassisted Childbirth Experiential Guide** and let my own journey support you in yours.

Chapter 3

BIRTH
Blissful Beginnings

"Like their animal sisters, women will someday deliver their own babies peacefully and painlessly at home. Women will understand that birth is only dangerous and painful for those who believe it is."
— **Laura Kaplan Shanley**, *Unassisted Childbirth*

With my first pregnancy, I was told my idea of a homebirth was both insidious and illegal, thus I dutifully registered with the prenatal clinic at the local hospital. Nobody mentioned the fact that hospital births have six times the mortality of home births.

Despite my obedience to this illegality rumor that I had no right to take my pregnancy and my child's birth into my own hands, a part of me clung tenaciously to the idea of birthing alone. Though I was exposed to the medical establishment on a regular basis, like a deviant school-girl, I had every intention of playing hooky on the eve of my daughter's birth.

In my last month of pregnancy I dreamed I would go into labor while dancing at the University pow wow, that my baby would be born into my arms with no intervention from anyone. I'll always remember my mounting excitement as the date of that pow wow drew near. As I headed out the door, putting the finishing touches on my dancing outfit, I packed a diaper bag for the first time in my life and felt like the Cinderella of Motherhood.

I entered the large, crowded auditorium just in time to catch the first drumming of the night. I quickly pulled my dancing shawl across my shoulders and headed happily to the dance floor. Just as I began my first turn, fringe from my shawl beginning its awesome flight, two hands gripped my arms and corresponding faces (my then-husband and a close friend) shamed me for such selfishness, insisting I was crazy to be so physically active late in my pregnancy.

Being stopped from participating in the unfolding of my dream was not nearly as shocking as the obedience I observed in me. Like a reprimanded child, I sat down and cried. Minutes later, a swelling sensation brought all my attention to the daughter within, and I realized labor had indeed begun.

By this time I had given over all of my power and heard myself mumbling to someone that I was having contractions. The next thing I knew, we were walking three miles in the snow, heading to the hospital where, upon arrival, my labor fizzled out and I was sent home. That night I lay crying in bed, holding my aching heart instead of my precious baby.

A week later I awoke at midnight to the sensation of warm water running between my legs. I calmly mentioned the wet bedding to my then-husband, and he frantically went running for the campus police. There I was, sitting in the back-seat of a police car which was heading to the last place I wanted to be.

Upon arrival at the much dreaded hospital site, I was coldly ordered into a wheelchair and taken up to the labor room. There, the nurses busted my water bag the rest of the way, probed around, then told me I was two centimeters and that it would be a while.

I got dressed and sought out the solitude I so desperately needed. For the next seven hours, while my then-husband slept on the waiting room couch, I stayed to myself — walking through the quiet three-story building, finding refuge in the emergency staircases, squatting deeply with each contraction and talking joyously to my womb-daughter the entire time.

At 7:00 am, I heard my name over the hospital intercom system, ordering me back to the labor room. Against my intuition I headed back to what became the epitome of my gullibility, as I proceeded to condone the initial command of intervention which led to a host of complications, resulting in a C-section.

Upon hearing my name over the intercom my first instinct had been to quietly exit the nearest door and walk home in the winter's chill where I could birth my baby in the privacy of my cozy travel-home. After all, no one would ever guess this pregnant and laboring woman was treking three miles in the snow to enjoy primal birthing in simple surroundings.

But I did not heed my inner call and I have a C-section scar to prove it. I'm not the only one wearing this badge of discourage, verification of a botched birth. This form of medical intrusion (the end result of all interventions prior) leads the way as the single most common major surgery in the United States. Between physicians and the pharmaceutical industry, childbirth is a fifteen billion dollar annual pelvic gold-mine.

Joseph Chilton Pearce, through his writings, has shown that, at the first sign of an interference or intervention of something that's liable to threaten a birthing mother, the mammalian limbic structures of the brain function to stop the birth process. The mother waits until the coast is clear or moves to another place to give birth where it's safer. That's our mammalian genetically-encoded heritage. When we succumb to hospital surroundings and the medical mentality we literally position ourselves to shut down progressive labor, which puts medical personnel on the aggressive and our true needs, as well as the needs of our unborn child, in jeopardy. I was experiencing regular and consistent contractions during my three-mile trek to the hospital the night of the pow wow, but the moment I walked through the metal doors of the emergency room my brain applied the brakes to the hormonal activity of my womb. And then, a week later, I experienced the same intelligent intervention by my brain when I was called back to the labor room after having spent seven glorious hours by myself. In both instances, I was, as Joseph Chilton Pearce describes, efforting to move to another place to give birth where it felt safer. Despite all my efforts, I was still in the psychic clutches of the medical mentality. Since hospital personnel are not trained to stay out of the way of Nature's plan, my desired birth — as well as the birthright of my daughter — was snatched away.

My long-yearned-for sovereign birth was wiped out in the flash of a surgeon's knife, preceded by the intruding foreplay of monitors, I7's, Pitocin, and the paranoid hands of total strangers. Right up until the final hour, when I was informed a C-section was the next step in this medical nightmare, I managed to maintain conscious contact with my daughter through each contraction.

I found labor itself to be a delightful challenge, despite the inhospitable environment of white-coated robots and the crass smell of sterility. Months prior, I had dreamed that a female deer would encourage me throughout the birth experience. Sure enough, with the first signs of labor came the vision of a beautiful doe standing in a snow-covered meadow. Her eyes were liquid pools of brown warmth and tranquility as she invited me to seek comfort with each contraction by looking deeply into the windows of her soul. At one point during my labor, when a nurse decided to speed up the Pitocin drip that caused my contractions to come nearly one atop the other — making it difficult to maintain my mental composure — the powerful doe reminded me to stay connected by gazing even more deeply into her eyes. When, due to the physical discomfort of medically-forced contractions I moved farther away from my center, this spotted doe mentor emphatically insisted I look down at her feet. I did. And to my complete amazement, out from the snowladen soil shot a breathtaking purple flower! I was so shocked by its sudden presence amidst the vision of winter I actually transcended the physical pain caused by medical technology.

Nonetheless, all of my mental work could not overturn the ugly consequences of medical intervention. I was in their clutches and my gullibility had placed me there, along with the codependent behavior of acquiescing to an unsupportive spouse whose fear-based mentality kept him from understanding my deep desire for a home birth. If only I had managed to defy his fears. If only I had educated myself about the procedural interventions practiced by hospital staff. My gullibility had led to giving my power away. I had "trusted" that the consciousness of the medical team was on my side and sensitive to my primal mothering needs. Instead, I learned the hard way that medical mentality and hospital procedures do not reflect the true needs of a birth in process. By allowing my then-husband to lead the way, and then stepping foot in that hospital, I assumed the patient/victim role, thereby sharing in the drama of a compromising birth where a total stranger in a white mask announced to me I had a baby girl, the same baby girl whose entrance into this world was both emotionally and physically painful, with an excruciatingly-long seven-hour wait before being united with her belly-slashed mother.

Why is it assumed that babies don't feel pain? The bright lights of a delivery room; total strangers grasping, pulling, scrubbing, probing, cutting, stabbing; unfamiliar voices devoid of emotion. As one psychologist reveals, "Pain makes a deep impression; babies are probably more impressionable than older children and adults. Protecting them from the impact of pain would prevent personal suffering at the beginning of life and the need for psychotherapeutic repairs later."

Part of the reason why I didn't have coverage on the birthing front of this battle to reveal my primal motherhood self was that all of my positive thinking and visualization efforts during pregnancy were geared toward manifesting a successful breastfeeding experience upon the birth of my daughter. Both my adoles-

cent and adult life had been riddled with shame over the small-
ness of my chest, a message which carried with it a feeling of
inevitable inadequacy regarding my mammalian self. This fear
of malfunction due to size was exacerbated by the many horror
stories from other mothers about failed nursing attempts,
cracked and bleeding nipples, and other unimaginable experiences in breastfeeding.

In an effort to protect myself from the flames of futility, I
joined La Leche League, an international organization with
groups all over the world designed to support breastfeeding
women. I performed daily visualizations. And I taped a beautiful picture of a mother nursing her baby onto my mirror where
I glanced at it frequently each and every day. I was diligent and
militant about coming to believe in my ability to nurse.

In retrospect, I can see I completely avoided educating myself
about or mentally preparing myself for the dynamics of birth.
At the time I did not comprehend the fact one cannot serve two
masters. Though my faith-filled heart was in favor of a self-
governing pregnancy and sovereign birth, my fearful head led
me in a different direction. I went to my prenatal appointments
punctually and had even once inquired about the birthing chair
at the hospital. I skipped the labor room/delivery room tour as
my way to prove earnestness to plans of birthing at home but
still, the majority of my actions were voting against my heart's
desire. Along the lines of Albert Einstein's advice that we cannot simultaneously prevent and prepare for war, I could not
simultaneously prevent and prepare for a hospital birth.

For the record, all my positive thinking and accompanying
mental work for a successful breastfeeding experience brought
to fruition my desired result. To this day, more than twelve
years later, I am still watching my children grow from the milk
my "small" breasts produce. Then again, I practiced no compromising behavior on this particular subject of primal mothering. I went to my La Leche League breastfeeding support meetings faithfully and made friends with breastfeeding women. I

never once succumbed to the advice of many who recommended I should have baby bottles and formula on hand, just in case my milk was nonexistent or insufficient. I burned all bridges and determined I would nurse my baby once she was born. Unfortunately, I had not pulled out all the stoppers for having her precious birth be as primal as her first feeding experience.

Like any recipe, it takes the inclusion and harmony of all ingredients to enact the finished product. My failed attempt at a primal birth was a perfect example of overlooking some of the necessary ingredients. Still, my first pregnancy did introduce me to the art of values clarification, putting first things first, and developing the daily discipline necessary to stay focused on important goals. These new virtues were carried into my second pregnancy where I learned more, and got better results.

I had never even heard of C-sections prior to the birth of my first child. Funny how I could have ignored what is a growing epidemic in today's society. I must have really been in denial on the subject of birth. Why did I unconsciously need to eliminate birth education from my pregnancy experience? This question stuck to me like glue. Six years later, when I learned I was pregnant again, the answer became crystal clear. My subconscious definition of birth was: big-time pain. I was afraid I had not the ability to endure the physical horror of a vaginal birth.

For six years I had worn the cloak of victim regarding my C-section, and the belief that the hospital staff simply did what needed to be done; it was inevitable; after all, I was inadequate in the way of birthing. I had bought the story-line that I was incapable of natural childbirth. But underneath this rationalization lived the forlorn female whose desire and need for a primal, sovereign birth still clung hopefully to her soul. Somewhere deep inside me I knew my hospital experience did not reflect my true abilities.

The moment I learned of this second pregnancy my heart immediately won over my head. I resolved to reach deep within and go to any lengths to create the birth I so desperately needed and wanted. I was hungry for the totality of my womanhood, and this time I would do my homework.

The first thing I did was contact an organization which supports women who are determined to experience a vaginal birth after a C-section (VBAC). In part because so many wanna-be surgeons (otherwise known as obstetricians) deem it only "natural" for C-section patients to experience more of the same; it is normal and prevalent for recipients of birth-surgery to experience the same in births to follow. I refused to pad the statistics.

My hospital experience had left such a sour taste in my mouth that I swung clear from seeking any medical assistance to securing a deep sense of sovereignty from start to finish.

The idea of a midwife didn't even register as a logical next step once I exorcised medical intervention from my psyche. I had seen how women gave themselves over to controlling midwives just as easily and obediently as when I had given my power away to hospital staff.

It was clear to me that my first major step toward a successful sovereign birth was to take responsibility for what had happened during the birth of little Sarah Lee. A victim mentality was not going to reap the rewards I desired. I had to disprove the notion that my C-section was necessary, and then ask myself why I gave my power away in the first place.

I remember the day my hospital chart came in the mail. A nurse-friend of mine interpreted the medical jargon for me and quickly analyzed that my C-section had been typical of those she sadly observed day in and day out on her job. Impatient medical staff trying to speed up the process of labor, creating compounding complications with each intervention which leads to further interventions resulting in major surgery. In other words, I had been medically raped.

At hearing the truth of my medical experience, my first reaction was not one of relief as I thought it would be. Instead, I cried deeply. The emotional pain was overwhelming. Somehow it had been easier, more comfortable, to believe I had succumbed to the inevitable and oh, what a good thing because the nice doctor had saved my baby! Now I was left with the raw realization that my much-desired primal birth, the prized treasure of my womanhood, had been at my fingertips and I let it slip away.

Why did I let it slip away? What beliefs had I clung to so tenaciously and unconsciously that their grip undermined the intensity of my desires? What fears about birth had I managed to sweep under the carpet? I certainly had my work cut out for me.

I began by taking full responsibility for my pregnancy; no prenatal exams, no back-up plans, no midwife contacts. I read books and articles written by women who experienced vaginal births after C-sections. I changed my reality around enough to be in alignment with my goal. Having learned the lesson that one cannot serve two masters, I put all my eggs in one basket and developed the courage necessary to envision this C-section-scarred body of mine bringing forth a healthy baby with no complications and no intervention.

I familiarized myself with the anatomy of birth and became increasingly interested in water birthing because, according to the testimonies I had read, pain in childbirth is decreased when laboring in water. Upon reading the book **Ocean Birth**, I chose this pregnancy as my motivation for getting to Hawaii.

I was finding out all about the responsibility that accompanies commitment and, as the time drew nearer, more obstacles seemed to cross my path helping me to release any hidden fears and other mental land-mines which needed unearthing before my due date. My biggest fear, probably the leading culprit which sent me reeling into denial with my first pregnancy, was my fear of pain. Just the idea of a baby passing through my cervix and beyond was enough to make me shudder. However, after reading **Painless Childbirth** by Fernand Lamaze and checking in more closely with my intuitive wisdom, I came to the joyous conclusion that pain was not a necessary component of childbirth.

I read everything I could get my hands on about pain; why it happens, how it happens, how to avoid it. I learned the importance of mind over matter. I knew from personal experience that pain could be eliminated simply by changing my mental focus, so I started a daily regime of birth visualizations where pain was non-existent. I also practiced some rebirthing techniques which got me in touch with the fact that my own mother had experienced excruciating pain during my forceps delivery. Her screams had become my reality about what to expect in childbirth.

With only two weeks to go in my pregnancy I was beginning to fret about the position of my daughter, as everyone was asking me the same question..."How do you know if your baby is in the right position to be born?" I began to have fear and called a midwife for the specific purpose of determining Jasmine's position. Instead of simply saying "Yes, she's head down," I endured a session of reprimand for having neglected to receive prenatal care, was told I was considered high risk because I had a previous C-section, I was nearly forty years old, and I was a red-head. She concluded her lecture with an offer to give me a discount by charging only one thousand dollars for the delivery service which she insisted I need.

As coincidences would have it, just as I was falling into the abyss of figuring how to come up with money to pay someone who had convinced me of my irresponsibility to birth alone, a very close friend happened to be driving by. He saw my car, slowed up, saw my face drained of its usual glow, and asked what was wrong. When I told him what was going on he replied, "So, you're going to bet one thousand dollars that your dream birth is not possible?" That gentle slap of reality spun my fully blossomed belly away from the midwife and toward the car that took me back to my special spot on the beach where a very special sovereign birth awaited.

A few nights later, an even stranger coincidence took place. While visiting with the same friend who had helped me flee from the fear-based clutches of that pushy midwife just days prior I had a dream in which Jasmine told me she preferred to be born up on the mountain of Kokee — which is where I happened to be at the time of this dream. She made it clear that negative consequences would surely result if I gave birth at the beach; strangers would interfere, and a whole new birthing nightmare would take place.

The next morning, while trying to digest this nocturnal demand from my womb-baby, the friend whose cabin I was visiting awoke to tell me Jasmine had come to him in a dream, showing her umbilical cord was adequate in length and when her head came out the first thing she would do is smile at him. She showed the birth taking place in a small cottage on the mountain of Kokee!

A few hours later I called a friend of mine in Oklahoma who, upon hearing my voice, immediately began telling me about this dream she had the night before...you guessed it. Jasmine was proudly telling her she was to be born in a cabin on a mountain in Hawaii.

Needless to say, I was in a state of confusion as I headed into the final days before labor began. With this new information I broke camp, left the beautiful sandy beach and guided my little family up the long and winding climb to Kokee Mountain. Three nights later I went into labor at my friend's cabin. I awoke to the feel of breaking waters, then quietly slipped from the bed and made myself comfortable in the kitchen. Wrapped in a green chenille bathrobe, I put on my earphones and began dancing while looking out at a most magnificent moon.

Things were fine until my friend woke up. When I disconnected from the dancing and told of my present laboring condition, fears of what I considered "inevitable pain to follow" began to surface and I worried about the fact that the ocean was beyond reach and my friend did not have a bath tub. Because I had not completely abandoned my idea of a waterbirth — because I still clung desperately to my fear of pain and used the waterbirth concept as insurance against it — my friend drove us to a neighboring cottage where awaited a deep bear-claw bath tub for my laboring and birthing needs.

Once settling into this new environment, I put my tape player and earphones to work again and disconnected from all that was going on around me. Contractions were five minutes apart as I resumed my birthing dance — a most beautiful sensual snake-like movement which I had been enjoying throughout my pregnancy. The physical environment of this neighbor woman's home was cozy, with a fire in the fireplace, candles and such, the smell of herb teas brewing...but something was wrong. There was an undercurrent of tension I intuitively felt was affecting the process of my labor. I felt like I was on stage as a flurry of activity surrounded me, people I didn't know coming and going, the telephone ringing, the television blaring, even a man attempting to get my attention in an effort to strike up a deal to buy my car! Next thing I knew, my contractions were weaker and farther apart.

Finally the neighbor woman suggested something must be wrong since so many hours had passed with no apparent progress. In my vulnerable state of mind that's all it took to start feeling my power slip away. Aside from the external distractions, up to this point I was indeed creating the experience I desired; no pain and lots of inner calm. In no time at all I managed to turn my will over to believing someone else must know more than I did.

This neighbor woman insisted my notion of a painless birth was unrealistic, birth was designed to be painful and I must accept that fact. In her words, "Giving birth is like shitting a watermelon." My fears were being fanned, and it wasn't too many contractions later that I began experiencing pain for the first time in over sixteen hours of joyous dancing and singing during labor.

I lost control. I couldn't regain my center. I found myself relying on others totally to keep me from falling into an abyss of physical horror. I had no idea who I was, where I was, nothing. I was being told to push, but I didn't believe in pushing. Out the window went my intuition, followed closely by my convictions. I lost connection to my own script. It seemed I could only do what I was told. I was in the midst of upholding the drama expected by society's consciousness — the sweating at the brow, all eyes on my perineum, coaching from the front and sidelines, hot packs between contractions. I knew instinctively that pushing was making things worse, but I had the bigger concern of being compliant amidst the coercion. The positions I was being told to assume were equally unnatural to my primal self. At one point I was accused of being stubborn about how things should go and, anyway, why couldn't I lie on my back and give birth like any other woman? Through all the submission on my part, I did manage to refuse to lie down.

In true form to things being "darkest" before the dawn, when I could endure the situation no longer, my friend who had saved me from the midwife's control just days prior took action. Up until this point he had been quietly yet uncomfortably staying in the background. All of a sudden he got right in my face and screamed above the chanting commands of his neighbor, "Hygeia, this is YOUR birth! YOU wanted it! Now, YOU take it!" His eyes burned conviction into mine and in the next moment I felt Jasmine swoop past my cervix and in five involuntary pushes she peeked her head of red hair out to smile at my friend — just as his dream had shown — then slid into homebase, safe, and soundless.

Unfortunately all the tension, awkward positions and forced pushing left me torn and tattered. Jasmine's exit through my vagina was my entrance to excruciating pain. Heavy laden with hemorrhoids, and stinging with every trip to the bathroom, the next few weeks were miserable. Yes, I had accomplished my vaginal birth after a C-section, but I had not achieved my ideal birth. Something was still missing.

With my first birth the uneasiness was vague because I claimed ignorance, plus I had been medicated prior to the surgery. At that time I had not educated myself about birth and I knew next to nothing about personal empowerment. Now, with this second birth, I was faced with the glaring facts: I had given away my power which resulted in a compromising birth experience. I experienced pain which I THOUGHT I didn't believe in, I pushed despite my intuition, and now it hurt to pee.

Once again, my ensuing reality was different from my original intent. There was obviously more to learn. This feeling of shame and disappointment clouded over me as I tried to pat myself on the back for a successful VBAC and a medically unassisted birth away from hospital personnel.

Two years later the question still burned in my mind. Would things have gone better if I had held onto my power? Could I have held onto my power under that peer-pressure circumstance?

Did I have to rip? Did it have to hurt? Unbeknownst to me, a third child was coming into my life and, as I watched the urine dipstick turn YES I thought to myself, maybe the third time is the charm.

Now came the task of giving myself full credit for having a VBAC under my belt rather than being the recipient of not one, but two C-section scars. I no longer had to jump the hoop of believing in my ability to birth. I had indeed experienced a medically unassisted vaginal homebirth. Though I had lost control and known fear in the latter part of those twenty-four hours of labor I had also succeeded in bringing forth my child. I had been courageous in the face of my fear.

After all, courage does not mean the elimination of fear. Courage means acting in spite of the fact that we are afraid. Even though there were no medications or monitors, no doctors or midwives, I still couldn't call my birthing experience "natural" because I saw nothing natural in the pain I felt, the pushing I performed, or the resulting physical assault on my perineum. My truly sovereign and primal birth was yet to be had.

With the sad taste of postpartum disappointment fresh in my mind I combed through every inch of that birth experience, resolving to overcome each obstacle that before had stood in my way. As I began to take full responsibility for all that had happened I was able to get a better view of my unconscious fears.

A part of me was afraid to be responsible for the outcome. I wanted somebody to blame, because deep down I believed I was incapable of a pleasant birth. Up until this moment of reflection and review I had indeed blamed outside circumstances for my compromising home birth. If only that woman had not said it was supposed to hurt. If only she had not insisted I push. If only there weren't so many people coming and going. From this blaming viewpoint I had no leverage with which to change my circumstances. But, when I considered the possibility I had unconsciously created the situation in the first place, I was then empowered with the option to change the nature of my personal reality.

Layer number one...I had no choice but to face my codependency issues. I was taking care of others during labor when I was supposed to be focusing on myself and my baby. During labor with my first pregnancy I had actually called from the hospital bed phone between contractions to order lunch for my husband who was sitting right there watching television! With my second laboring experience I was concerned over the fact I was taking up someone else's bed and causing inconvenience to others; a bed, by the way, I never would have been sitting on had I not listened to the bed-owner's motto that laboring women belonged there.

Like my grief over the unnecessary interventions with my first daughter's birth, I now faced the truth that I had, once again, foisted my efforts to have a sovereign and complication-free birth experience. I had rationalized I could not have done it without those people at that mountain cottage. It was just now occurring to me I may have needed them simply because they were there. When we are alone in a given endeavor and there's nobody to turn to, we are pressured to reach within for the strength and stamina to carry us through. After all, that's why vision quests are a solitary dance. Who is to say I would have failed in solitude?

Less than two years later, with a third child growing peacefully inside my womb, this revelation from my second birth experience was accompanied by a burst of self-confidence which put me on course for that 100% commitment needed to finally know the primal birth defined by my heart and soul.

As coincidence would have it, the day I reached maximum throttle with this non-negotiable level of commitment I received in the mail a newsletter which supported unassisted homebirth. I immediately ordered the book **Unassisted Childbirth** by Laura Kaplan Shanley which was highly recommended by the editors of this particular newsletter.

Laura's book became my bible. I read it repeatedly, studied it, slept with it under my pillow, and devoured every resource book suggested by the author. This woman knew what I wanted! What I needed! Nobody up to that point understood why I would want to give birth all by myself. Laura Kaplan Shanley had enjoyed her first two births in the presence of her partner, but realized that, for her, birth was a personal challenge she would rather reach — like a vision quest — alone. Someone was speaking my language. I finally felt safe inside myself because I was no longer alone.

Most of the medically unassisted homebirths I was reading about in other books were stories where women endured intense levels and long hours of pain, giving all credit for success to their partner, saying they couldn't have done it without his support. Each testimony I read brought back to mind that recent revelation...maybe I needed those people at that cottage simply because they were there. I know I can change a flat tire with more conviction and efficiency when there is not someone, especially a man, nearby. No, I wanted to birth alone and, like Laura Kaplan Shanley learned for herself, personal empowerment was the reward which awaited me.

I soon found out how few people agreed with or supported my birthing intentions. My friends took on the form of fear-based worry-warts and neighbors shunned me for bringing such craziness upon the community. I created a support team, a Mastermind Group which consisted of Laura's wisdom inside her book, the powerful speaker Les Brown inside his cassette tape series **Live Your Dreams**, and Susan Jeffers inside her book **Feel The Fear And Do It Anyway!** Though I couldn't realistically invite my trusted team over for tea on any given afternoon, the close psychic connection I maintained with these empowered role models kept me going as I blasted through all the obstacles necessary for creating a totally successful, totally sovereign, totally primal birth.

In the Big Book of Alcoholics Anonymous it says, "We will not regret the past nor wish to shut the door on it." Relating this wisdom to my situation, I had to forgive myself and others for my previous birth experiences. I had to heal from all the blame and any of the shame. I took responsibility for the fears and other beliefs that led me to making the decisions that created my experiences. I asked my dreams to show me how those births would have gone if those fears didn't exist inside me. From this introspective homework assignment came a sense of peace. The past was now a rich treasure of self-understanding, no longer a slaughter-ground where my dream was twice crucified.

I looked beyond the birth of Matthew to the beautiful bonding between myself and my three precious children. I learned to be patient, embracing the idea that patience was a creative waiting, trusting that in time what I desired would come to pass.

Unearthing my hidden belief systems was not an overnight job. Gestation was happening on all levels, not just in-utero. I had several dreams about premature birth and I knew that these

nocturnal premonitions were my cue to accept patience as a nurturing and necessary virtue for the overall success of my desired
sovereign birth. My impatience was mostly tied into my
increasing intolerance of the chatter-box in my head telling me
that I would fail and all would suffer as a result. I wanted to get
past the finish-line as soon as possible so I no longer had to live
with the anxiety of apprehension.

Then came the hoop with the most flames lapping within. All
of this inner work would be in vain were I not to activate the
peristaltic motion of emotional cleansing, flushed only by the
act of forgiveness. I had to learn that forgiving is a choice I
make — a gift I give to somebody even if they don't deserve it.
I had to heal my heart from blame by forgiving myself, as well
as forgiving others who weren't to blame in the first place.

This was really hard for me. But I wanted this heartfelt birth
no matter what, and I had to pay the price. I had been blaming
my ex-husband for first whisking me off the dance-floor and
then again for flagging down the cop who ran red lights to get
me to a hospital where I endured a C-section. And I had been
blaming the take-charge woman whose cottage I borrowed
while giving birth to Jasmine. The cycle of blame had to stop
some time. And NOW was the time.

I had a vested interest in blame. It kept me free from self-
responsibility. In **The Celestine Prophecy** James Redfield
writes, "Subtle and ever-present, core beliefs are invisible
determining factors in our lives. These thoughts imperceptibly
organize our internal field and determine our continuing reality." Working with the twelve steps for personal empowerment
originally created by members of Alcoholics Anonymous, I rec-
ognized my seeming powerlessness over the compulsion to
blame. With pen in hand, I made a list of all the people, places,
and institutions I had blamed for my past birth experiences.

I set out to make the contacts necessary for my healing. It
wasn't easy nor was it impossible. I had a bigger YES burning
inside. I felt so empowered and light-hearted after making these

amends, and was surprised at the gravity of weight which had accompanied my previous grudges.

With diligence to weeding my mental garden throughout this third pregnancy, the only fear that remained was a concern for environmental cleanliness at the time of Matthew's birth. Each story of unassisted homebirth I had read about included the component of sterile sheets, sterilized scissors, rubbing alcohol, etc. Was this really necessary? My intuition whispered NO. Then I thought about all the primal women on the planet who, on this very day, were giving birth near rice paddies or wherever else their daily tasks took them. I reflected on the mother cat who brings her litter into a world of old clothes in a wicker basket, or the dreamy-eyed mare whose foal drops gently to an unsterile ground. I concluded my usual standard of domestic cleanliness was sufficient.

For a couple of days I went in and out of labor. My contractions were extremely pleasant and affirming to my heart. I was indeed heading into the luxury of my dream birth. As a way to increase my tolerance for physical intensity — and to protect my perineum from tearing this time — I massaged myself with olive oil and, via this gentle stimulation, enjoyed several wonderful orgasms throughout the day.

After putting my girls to bed for the night, I poured a glass of organic grape juice and curled up in my overstuffed rocker. Staring out at the magnificent ocean view, I resumed perineal massage and reached orgasm with every contraction. Nothing in my life had ever compared to this moment in time. In my journal I wrote, "I'm massaging myself with olive oil and enjoying the most expansive orgasms I have ever known. Sex has never compared to the sensual pleasure I am experiencing right now. Each uterine hug is so big and beautiful. I love watching my belly rise rhythmically and then relax. Matthew's hugs from my womb are truly one on top of the other, with little or no break between them. Damn, this feels good! I feel a sudden urge to take a hot bath by candlelight. Be back soon."

Within moments of slipping into the soothing water I experienced two eye-opening contractions which suggested I was much farther along than I realized. A sudden urge to sit on the toilet was immediately followed by the breaking of my waters.

I was confused. With my first two pregnancies my water initially broke, and then was followed by twenty-four hours of labor. Despite my intention to enjoy a quick and easy birth this time around, I had still evidently hung onto the belief I would labor for twenty-four hours after my water broke, as I had done two times prior. This did not feel like the beginning of labor.

All of a sudden I felt overwhelmed. I was treading on unfamiliar territory. I knew I better make some quick decisions...did I want to give birth in the bath tub? Did I want to wake up my daughters? A few months prior I had dreamed eight-year-old Sarah Lee was holding her brother's head as he was coming out. As a homeschooling mother I am always on the prowl for "real life" experiences to share with my children, so it only made sense to wake them up.

I barely had time to rouse my daughters from their slumber. We all hurried into the living room where I threw a plastic sheet on the carpet, got down on all fours, and observed my body assist passively as Matthew slid out quickly and, true to my dream's preview, Sarah Lee guided her baby brother as he descended to the living-room floor. Determined to participate in this magnificent event, two-year-old Jasmine yelled, "I'll get a rag and clean him up!" as she went running for the kitchen towel.

Moments later we all hopped back in the tub and waited for the cutting of his umbilical cord. I simply snipped it with a pair of non-sterilized sewing scissors and didn't clamp off the ends — I have yet to observe a cat, dog, or horse doing so.

When we got out of the tub the girls sat in the rocker while I wrapped Matthew up for them to hold. As I was passing him over I felt a swoop, and reached down just in time to catch my placenta before it splattered all over the beige carpet. A trip to the bathroom revealed the rewards of my relaxed birthing experience...my perineum was COMPLETELY INTACT. No vaginal tears, no pain, not even a whisper of discomfort. There had been no pain throughout my day of labor, during the birth itself, or afterward. I was in heaven because the gates of heaven existed inside myself. My dream had come true because I had created its reality.

I was also finally realizing just how devastated I had felt by the perineal damage incurred with Jasmine's birth, and furthermore by the blinding pain of my slashed belly when Sarah Lee was born. Now, instead of directing part of my attention toward a bleeding hemorrhoid-laden crotch or stapled abdomen, I was placing all my energy onto my peaceful newborn and my mesmerized daughters.

A few hours later we all crawled into our family bed and slept gracefully until awakening for our usual morning walk to the health-food store, where Matthew was placed on the produce scale to register a beautifully compact 6 pounds, 14 ounces.

There were lots of rainbows that morning — or were there? Maybe they resided in me, thus that was all I could see. It was the most magical day of my life, me and all those other primal mothers on the planet birthing beautifully and carrying on.

I had found the power within to make my dream come true.

Choose a joyously primal birth, then begin to weed your mental garden of any and all fears which may separate you from your primal bliss.

Chapter 4

BONDING
Bringing It All Together

"All babies look forward to a womb with a view."
— **Ashley Montagu,** *Touching: The Human Significance of the Skin*

For nine months our babies listened to the rhythmic activity of our heartbeats and oh how they love, upon birth, to be placed at our chest where they re-connect to the beautiful sound of mother's rhythmic song.

Human babies need to be held. We are a continuous contact species, biologically designed to feel the warm embrace of our provider, the tactile stimulation derived from touch. Postpartum depression is non-existent for the mother who clings tenaciously to her newborn upon birth. The biological needs of both are intertwined and, when those combined needs are being met, babies don't cry and mothers aren't depressed.

A baby's cry is their only avenue for signaling a need to be held. They cry to be picked up. There is actual physical pain for babies who are deprived of the stimulation derived from touch. Society has a hang-up about giving babies what they need. We've all heard the admonition, "Don't pick the baby up or she'll control you by crying every time she wants to be held" or "Let him cry, it's good for his lungs." Wouldn't such a mentality then suggest bleeding is good for the veins?

The human being is the slowest growing of all species. We're absolutely helpless in the first year, save our ability to communicate needs through crying. When those cries are not heard, are instead reacted to with neglect, abuse, or tangible placebos like food, television, toys and other devices, then our babies learn to bond with an artificial alternative to the human connection.

The consumer industry is filled with products which attempt to be mommy. Don't buy devices to simulate what is real. Rather than wind up a baby swing, let your infants feel the rhythmic motion of your active body as they rest peacefully against you. Recognize the symbiosis between you and your young. A strong bond will take you through rough times.

I remember walking down Main Street at midnight on a snowy Oklahoma night. One-month-old Sarah Lee felt restless and I didn't have the floor space in a 20-foot travel trailer to walk her back and forth. So I put her in the baby sling and the rocking, rhythmic motion of my active body sent her into a sweet slumber while I enjoyed a moonlight stroll. Vimala McClure, author of **Tao Of Motherhood** reminds us, "A mother who gives herself completely to her infant meets herself in the dark and finds fulfillment. In the hours between midnight and dawn, she crosses the threshold of self-concern and discovers a Self which has no limits. A wise mother meets this Presence with humility and steps through time into selflessness. Infants know when their mothers have done this, and they become peaceful."

Bonding to something other than mommy is fertile ground for a compromising childhood, a turbulent adolescence, and an addiction-oriented adulthood. My most vivid memories as a toddler were the many nights I slipped quietly into the kitchen, grabbed a hand full of white Wonder bread and sneaked back to my lonely bed where I sucked on slice after slice until I would lull myself to sleep. Such bonding to food has led me through a myriad of eating disorders throughout my life. We are destined to bond and if not to our mothers, then to whatever is within our reach.

Children have a right to their mothers, and a woman has the right to bond with her children regardless of her financial or relationship status. Unfortunately the term "illegitimate" is still present in the consciousness of our culture. Single women who choose to follow through with pregnancies and end up on the welfare rolls automatically enter the lion's den of social disapproval, and their offspring are considered exempt from needing a full-time mommy beyond a certain age. Being born out-of-wedlock is hardly a disease that taints the potential of our children. Leonardo Da Vinci, age twelve and illegitimate, vowed "I shall become one of the greatest artists the world has ever known and one day I shall live with kings and walk with princes." Let's not forget welfare constitutes only one percent of the annual government spending, and I am personally much more interested in helping single women raise peaceful humanitarians than I am to motivate the military into building yet another bomb, or encouraging politicians to scout out other planets. In the June 20, 1994 issue of **Time** magazine the headlines read, "The War on Welfare Mothers: Reform may put them to work, but will it discourage illegitimacy?" Once again, the insinuation is being made that children born exclusively into the arms and lives of their mothers are social deviants.

The only way to discourage "illegitimacy" is to encourage codependency recovery because, in most cases, mothers end up single by virtue of the fact they repeat patterns in relationships which lead to the same results over and over again. I suggest welfare reform which teaches attachment mothering along with psychological counseling to overcome dysfunctional parenting practices and codependency recovery support, all culminating in a home business training program which includes a start-up grant or guaranteed small business loan making a bridge between welfare support and economic independence.

Not only does society create a wedge between mother and

child by day, but night-time is equally influenced by cultural attitudes. The family bed is a concept in bonding seldom practiced in our culture. The Western practice of placing babies in their own beds at night is at odds with human nature. Given the fact infants experience hunger at night as well as during the day, not to mention the fact emotional security for infants is found in suckling (oral gratification), it only makes sense that physical closeness between mother and child would continue into the night.

Simply rolling over to breastfeed creates convenience for the mother and comfort for her offspring. A friend called me one morning to say she was completely exhausted from sleepless nights since her baby's birth four days prior. I asked if she was sleeping with her baby. She seemed surprised by my inquiry, as she saw no correlation between her sleep deprivation and the baby's place of slumber. I suggested she bring the baby to bed with her. The next morning she called me and in a most ecstatic voice reported, "It worked! I feel great! I just nursed him right there in bed and neither one of us needed to fully wake up. Thanks so much for the suggestion!"

Our babies naturally root for our breasts when they are hungry or insecure. They might make little grunting sounds in their search, but if we are close by to respond promptly there is no need for them to come fully alert through the distress signal.

The two most popular arguments against family bed go like this..."You might roll over and suffocate your baby" and "You'll spoil him and never get him to sleep in his own bed." First, the human species would have snuffed itself out thousands of years ago if infant suffocation were the result of family sleeping arrangements. Like all aspects of the modern world, cribs and separate sleeping quarters are new in light of our rich heritage in nocturnal togetherness. Second, I know of not a single case where older children clamor to remain in bed with their parents.

Older children eventually get to a point in their young lives when they want to seek privacy during times of slumber. In part, it has to do with their developing sexuality and a desire to enjoy privacy during masturbation. When Sarah Lee was ten years old she went through phases where she excitedly created a comfortable bed in her art-room and actually slept there for a few nights, soon to be followed by another dose of the family bed where back came her horsey blanket and angel pillow. Toward the end of her eleventh year she began spending most of her nights in her own bedroom, yet always fully aware of the fact that she is welcome into the family bed whenever she feels the need. It's fun to allow our children the free reign to travel what trails their hearts require. And it's fun to wake up to a bunch of warm bodies who make up your sacred family unit!

And then there's the insidious idea that the family bed is a hot-seat for incest. Nothing could be farther from the truth. I have listened time and again to incest survivors describe how the adults they trusted slipped silently into the private bedrooms of these once-children where nobody was around to protect them from the perpetrator's plan. The safest place for our children is that empty space right next to us as we sleep. The family bed gives intimacy a higher meaning as our babies and young children feel our affection AND our protection.

The most common reason why aspiring primal mothers don't sleep with their babies is due to what I call "spousal pouting," partners who feel threatened by the presence of a baby in the parents' bed. Primal mothering requires the ability to defend the emotional needs and biological rights of our children, despite any argument from others. We are not sex or cuddle machines designed to be ready at the call of our lovers. We are hormonal and heartfelt female humans looking after the needs of our offspring.

Night-time bonding is easily available because we all go to bed at the end of our day. But the bonding process itself is a round-the-clock responsibility. How do we meet our financial obligations, run errands, clean house, and pursue personal goals while tending to the continuous contact needs of our young? We see pictures of the baby strapped on its mother's back while a woman works in the rice paddies, but what does that have to do with our modern world?

The concept of baby-wearing in a culture where mother-child separation is the norm creates the need to train ourselves to break past social ignorance, that we may embrace the simplicity and convenience of continuous contact. People will always have an opinion to offer, especially the dangerous notion that we are spoiling our young by not disciplining them to be apart from us. But the truth of the matter is that a most beautiful kind of discipline develops in our babies as they observe the world from their secure place on our body. They are calm, quiet, and alert. That's discipline.

Marsupial mothering, the act of baby-wearing, gives our children a leading edge in intellectual growth as well as a warm, cozy place against our body. For my graduate thesis I interviewed a neurosurgeon at Tulane University who gave me this advice regarding my business of making and distributing baby slings. He said, "Keep beating the path because baby slings offer the single most successful method for optimum neurological development."

The constant rocking motion derived from our active body actually stimulates our baby's brain, especially the part of the brain where pleasure is produced. This explains why baby-sling babies always appear in a state of bliss. They are!

Prior to Sarah Lee's birth I knew nothing about baby slings. My plan was to use a Native American cradleboard. But one night I had a dream which sent me in a new direction. In the dream I was exchanging the wooden cradleboard in for a beautiful piece of purple cloth to be used for wearing my newborn. Acknowledging the message in my dream opened my eyes and my imagination to the ancient art of baby-wearing. With my newborn tucked securely in her purple cloth — her womb with a view — I could easily wash and hang clothes, attend my college classes, lecture at conferences, buy groceries, sew slings for other mothers to enjoy, type up articles, clean my house, prepare meals, exercise and whatever else I needed to do in a given day.

In my cross-cultural research I came to appreciate the physiological and psychological benefits of marsupial mothering. Cultures where babies are worn for up to three years host higher rates of social peace than societies where babies are relegated to cribs and other non-human holding devices. Studies with premature babies who received consistent rhythmic motion have shown quicker weight gain. Rhythmic motion gave them the chance to feel in-utero stimulus, otherwise denied them as a result of being born prematurely.

My baby didn't cry. She had everything she needed: physical warmth, closeness, skin contact, the sound of my happy heart, nursing access, and the world in which to observe from her safe pouch. I didn't have to stop everything I was doing in order to feed her, I just hooked her up and kept on going. The close proximity of baby to breast allowed for frequent nursings, which in turn resulted in a greater milk supply.

The primary purpose of my home business, Mother And Child Reunion is to establish in mothers and newborns their rightful couple-ship. These past twelve years have been blessed with equipping thousands of women with our Affordable Cozy Cradle baby slings, and receiving beautiful testimonies such as the ones to follow:

"Your Cozy Cradle has saved me from distress. I really can't put into words what the 'cozy' has meant to me and my baby. It seems so simple, so right, so natural to keep my baby close and secure."

"I love my new Cozy Cradle so much! It is so lovingly made with the ribbon and teething beads, and I wear it everywhere."

"I enjoy wearing my 5-week-old son when he nurses. I can nurse discreetly in the mall, in restaurants, wherever! And he sleeps so soundly nestled to my breast after feeding. I've found the Cozy Cradle works great when he's fussy; the movement and my heartbeat seems to calm him right down."

"Carrying my child close to my heart enables me to dive into this young soul's reality and know her needs, while being free to carry on with my own life. It is the best way to ensure mutual respect and love to both mother and child."

"My Cozy Cradle allows me to hold my baby close while I get my chores done. I can breastfeed her, sing to her, and rock her to sleep while my hands are free. She is easily comforted in her Cozy Cradle and prefers to nap in it. I like knowing she is warm, content, and not alone. This keeps us both happy, as she is held close to me where she can see things and I have my hands free, and my arms don't get sore from her weight."

"I can actually wear my twins! Now I don't need to choose one baby over the other. When they both need comforting, I can carry them each in a Cozy Cradle and snuggle them at the same time, while I still have the freedom to walk around and use both my hands. Thanks for making life a little easier."

Happily nurtured babies are content babies. Though there are many reasons why child abuse and neglect occurs, one contributing factor is the stress and intolerance a mother can feel when her baby cries a lot. Sleeping with our children at night and wearing our babies during the day creates such a peaceful environment there's little room for stress.

One very important beauty of baby-wearing is that we are offering our children a bird's-eye view of life. Quiet alertness is their reality as they move with us from task to task. Our hands and arms are free to perform those functions being observed by our infants. At present, our culture chooses one of two options: either a mother gives up trying to accomplish much and just holds her baby while awkwardly attempting a few things, or the baby is relegated to a crib or other artificial holding device so the mother can be productive in various areas of her daily life.

One of my favorite reasons for wearing my babies is so other people don't insist on holding them. Part of the bonding process is for my baby to feel safe in familiar arms, gazing into familiar eyes. With my baby tucked comfortably against me, people admire without insisting on holding my young. If they do ask, I simply tell them, "No, my baby is only family-held."

Postpartum moments/months are so intimate, and we are responsible for respecting that sacred space, regardless of the opinion of others. People have accused me of being selfish and overprotective because I don't let anyone outside my immediate family hold my babies until they are several months old; and even then I watch closely for my baby's reaction — taking them back immediately if they appear the least bit insecure or uncomfortable. These are MY children, and I must follow MY protective instincts.

I once asked a woman who ordered my baby sling what she liked best about wearing her baby. She said, "I like to wear my baby because then I am assured that nobody will steal her." This response was probably instigated by the sad fact that, just days prior at the local grocery store, a baby left in his plastic carrier on the grocery cart was stolen while the mother was looking the other way. Such a nightmare could never occur in the life of a marsupial mother.

Plastic carriers and strollers don't give our infants the human touch they need. And for us mothers, it's far more cumbersome to carry one of those plastic devices or to steer a stroller over curbs and through pedestrian traffic than it is to enjoy the physical warmth of a blissful babe against our body. We just never know when having our hands free and our child safely secured to us could help save the life of our family.

A tornado in Oklahoma sent me running for shelter, belongings in each hand, while Sarah Lee was safe in the sling. A hurricane in Hawaii found me wearing both of my daughters as I gathered up material necessities with my free hands and sought safety from our home's nearing demise. In both cases, my mental energies were freed up to deal with the situation at hand instead of feeling overwhelmed by trying to keep a handle on frightened, insecure children.

Bonding begins at conception. On the spiritual and biological levels we begin to form a relationship with our developing child. This is also the time to begin groundwork for maintaining the bonding process after birth. With our baby tucked conveniently inside us we have yet to be faced with the challenge of accomplishing daily responsibilities alongside the moment-by-moment needs of a newborn.

With each of my pregnancies I quickly created a blueprint and worked diligently throughout those months of gestation to build a lifestyle reflective of my desire. With the cornerstone being my commitment to mother/child togetherness, the construction of a lifestyle conducive to primal mothering went smoothly and the finished product was always forthcoming.

For instance, when I moved to Hawaii in preparation for my second birth, I applied for government housing assistance the same day I purchased a tent built for two. I invested in the future while tending to the present. The lady at the housing program informed me their waiting list was at least two years long. Still, I added my name to that list and continued to envision a satisfactory home environment for my expanding family, though at the time I wasn't sure if that meant a cute little cottage or the eventual purchase of a larger tent. Four days before Jasmine was born I received a letter stating my name had reached the top of the list and we were now eligible to move into a two-bedroom home.

All dreams have a price. Maintaining togetherness with my children has meant sacrificing many things. But, not living my dream has an even bigger price. In all decisions I ask myself how I want the story to tell ten years from now — "I wanted to be with you, but..." or "I stayed with you, no matter what."

Primal mothering is a crash course in values clarification. I am faced with making choices at every turn, choices that will mold the future reality of my family. Staying loyal to my policy of togetherness brings about tremendous feelings of confidence, despite the environmental discomfort we occasionally know.

A path always seems to be made, so long as I keep true to my commitment. The following message from German philosopher Johann Wolfgang von Goethe eloquently emphasizes the attitude I came to adopt, in order to live my dream on a daily basis...

"Until one is committed
there is hesitancy, the chance to draw back,
always ineffectiveness.
Concerning all acts of initiative
there is one elementary truth,
the ignorance of which kills countless ideas
and splendid plans:
That the moment one definitely commits oneself,
then providence moves too.
All sorts of things occur to help one
that would otherwise never have occurred.
A whole stream of events issues from the decision,
raising in one's favor all manner
of unforeseen incidents and meetings
and material assistance,
which no wo/man could have dreamt would have come
her/his way."

Many times, what appeared to be obstacles turned out to be opportunities which led me into more enjoyable dimensions of living. During my college days, with two classes remaining to complete graduate school, I encountered resistance from a professor who — unlike those for two years prior — refused to allow my baby-wearing self into his class. I was placed in a position of making a choice between my upcoming graduate degree or maintaining the mother/child bond. With Sarah Lee at my breast, serenity in my heart, and faith in our future I turned away from the choice to compromise, walked out of the professor's office, glided down the thick wooden steps of the social science building, and strode confidently away from the university.

Three days later, while reading the best-selling book **Fit For Life** I learned of a doctoral program in Natural Nutrition which could be achieved, in most part, through correspondence. Upon applying to the Life Science Institute at Austin, Texas and submitting my graduate thesis, I soon heard back from the president, T.C. Fry. This honorable man was so impressed with my thesis he offered me a full tuition scholarship along with a writing assistantship to develop a Natural Mothering curriculum.

My future reality would have been COMPLETELY different, not to mention vividly compromising, had I opted to adhere to the condescending demands of that professor and obediently turned little Sarah Lee over to someone else while attending his mandatory classes. Yes, Richard Bach, it's true. The only thing that shatters dreams is compromise.

Another interesting turn of events which came my way via honoring togetherness, the cornerstone of primal mothering, was when I gave up what little help I was getting from public assistance. When Sarah Lee was just a toddler it was mandatory that I enter a work-training program whereby I was to place my daughter in day-care eight hours daily for a week while I was to attend this workshop. At the time I was working diligently on my graduate thesis, building my baby sling business, and writing articles for various mothering publications along with feeding the vision for writing this book. Despite my heroic efforts at developing a solid financial base, the welfare worker insisted my responsibility rested in entering the work-force as soon as possible. Sensing the coldness of this woman, Sarah Lee crawled into my lap and sought comfort in nursing, to which the worker responded, "And you better wean that child because we ARE going to put you out on a job!"

Our housing was on the line. Without welfare's financial

assistance I would not be able to pay rent. I LIKED having a roof over our head, but I LOVED being with my child.

I thanked the welfare worker for what assistance I had thus far received, drove over to the realty office where I gave notice on my apartment, and went home to sew up a hefty supply of baby slings, change the oil in my car, pack up our belongings, and set forth on an adventure which led us through three months of delightful travel. We drove throughout the southwestern states selling slings to mothers we met along the way. We thoroughly enjoyed the priority of our relationship despite the fact that never once did we have more than a quarter of a tank of gas in the car or $5.00 in our pockets. We were literally fueled on faith, while managing to keep our fruit bowl filled.

We need welfare reform which takes into consideration both the bonding needs of children and the career needs of women. There is great social hostility toward mothers who choose welfare as an avenue of support. Even the welfare workers themselves often exude a condescending attitude toward those of us seeking assistance. Welfare needs to move away from a punitive attitude and instead adopt an encouraging vision of its recipients. For instance, rather than handicap female graduate students by considering them "work eligible" because they hold an undergraduate degree, instead encourage mothers to remain on welfare and pursue higher levels of education which can ultimately place them in higher paying and more rewarding careers. Any financial assistance program holding the idea that a toddler is old enough to be separated from us is not taking into account the true needs of our upright and walking older babies.

A primal mother does what it takes to stay with her young, like that Mexican woman whose collection can was in charge of procuring family finances while her baby held firm to his rightful place.

Perhaps the most joyful benefit of togetherness is the storehouse of memories which become inscribed on the family script. Sarah Lee and I are especially fond of the warm, fuzzy

feelings we get over the "curb-side canned corn" memory when
sometimes that was the only meal we could afford. Our financially hardest times came during those months when we lived
on the beaches of Hawaii. Without a sewing machine, I could-
n't make and sell baby slings. Sarah Lee took it upon herself to
get up early in the morning, paint beautiful pictures, then go sell
them to the tourists who visited the beach near where our tent
was pitched. This six-year-old entrepreneur and devoted family
member was averaging five dollars a day! After replenishing
her art supplies, she put the rest in my purse for our daily trip to
the nearest store which was more than two miles away. There,
we bought two cans of corn and sat on the curb-side. Using our
trusty knife, we opened those prized packages and proceeded to
relish each sweet and succulent morsel of that meal. To this day,
the mere sight of a can of corn melts my heart to the core!

Another benefit of following our dreams is the positive
impact it inevitably has on others. We become a role model of
conviction, a light which shows the way for others who consider living a life of commitment rather than merely an existence
of compromise. I often think of my friend who sadly weaned
her infant and went back to work as a breastfeeding advocate
for the government WIC program. She was in a position to
make some positive changes for the future of mothers and children, had she chosen a path different than day-care. How different the rippling effects would have been had she tucked her
sweet, deserving daughter into a sling and reported back to
work. Her mothering convictions amidst career competency
could have influenced her co-workers, government policy,
social consciousness, and thus the world at large. Instead, she
fanned the notion that mother-child separation was inevitable.
It's a supply and demand world out there. If we demand a society where the needs of our children are included in all decision
making, then we will ultimately be supplied with an environment conducive to primal mothering. I envision a future where
all architectural blueprints include the needs of mothers and

their children. Sound-proof enclosures in college classrooms where mothers can hear the lecture while rocking their babies. Public rest-rooms with little sinks and toilet seats along with changing tables and rocking chairs. Twelve-step recovery groups with play areas for children of all ages.

How did society get to the place where handing over our babies is the norm? Maybe it's a sad by-product of the way we hand over our pregnancies and our births. Do you remember being told as a child not to disturb the freshly-hatched birdlings, or the family cat with her new litter of kittens? Do you remember why? That the mothers might abandon their young if they smell the scent of another on their offspring...

When strangers surround us during birth and then remove our newborn from our sight, smell, and touch; when still more strangers scrub away the primal scent of our baby's natural sweet covering known as vernix, and when these strangers return our baby to us many minutes or even hours later...this is a gross act of interference with the postnatal bonding process.

As primal mothers we are assigned the task of protecting the mother/child bond through all its stages. Finances are obviously one of the biggest obstacles we face, since the business world does not invite our children to the work-place. A great option to consider is creating a home business. I started my baby sling business by collecting enough aluminum cans to put ten dollars down on a used sewing machine. I sewed up one sling, sold it to a friend who requested it for her infant son, then used her payment to buy enough fabric to make two more slings which sold at the next La Leche League meeting. Within a month the sewing machine was paid off and I had made enough profit to pay for an ad in La Leche League's bi-monthly magazine, **New Beginnings**. That was twelve years ago. I'm still happily in the baby sling business and have added book-writing, newsletter production, fitness video tapes, motivational cassette tapes, natural nutrition consultation, and commodities trading to my home-based career. All of this in the context of raising my three beautiful children.

We live in a time when the mother/child bonding relationship is being crucified at every stage. We need supportive people in our lives, people who agree with us that nothing is more important than the time we spend with our children. During the time Sarah Lee and I traveled the southwest I met with the staff at **Mothering** magazine in Santa Fe, New Mexico — a business place, by the way, that welcomes both their employees and the children of those employees. When Peggy O'Mara, the publisher/editor of this powerfully nurturing magazine, learned I was living out of my car, and therefore without access to electricity for sewing my slings, she offered me her personal office as a place to replenish my supply.

In one of her editorial letters, Peggy O'Mara once said that demanding premature independence in our young is like begrudging winter for not yet being spring. But so much of what we do to our children is a repetition of the parenting we received.

Just as a computer will only retrieve what is stored in memory, we must pull up the file on our past, edit where necessary, and re-program ourselves so future generations can enjoy a higher state of self-love and peaceful co-habitation. Each and every one of the baby slings I make hosts a ribbon of seven colorful beads representing the Native American philosophy that our decisions today must be based on their overall impact seven generations from now. Will tomorrow be the fruition of humanity's dream to develop into the cosmic beings we are intended to be, or a nightmare which continues to haunt us all?

I once had a nightmare which affected me so much, when I woke up I was drenched in cold sweat and frightened to the core. In the dream, it was a rainy night, around midnight. A huge sign was flashing the words DRIVE-UP DAYCARE. I watched a car pull up to the side of the cold, gray building where a large metal drawer opened out. The woman in the car deposited her two small, sleeping children into this holding-tank, tore off a ticket stub, rolled her window up against the rain, and drove away into the night. I stood there and felt nausea overtake my entire being. The dark, cold, and wet night seemed to say it all as I wept for humanity's fate.

Dreams give us the great benefit of changing priorities in the middle of the stream. Even a computer will ask if you are sure before deleting a file. Sad outcomes are simply the by-product of repeated treks down paths which deny the necessary nurturing of humanity. The decision to govern our own pregnancy, enjoy the privacy of birth, remain with our babies, feed them from the nutritious divinity of our breasts, wear them close as we carry on in daily life, sleep together in a warm and secure embrace, and give ourselves over to the primal instinct in all areas of our mothering experience lays the golden bricks which pave the way for a better world to come.

Chapter 5

BREASTFEEDING
Best Food, Beautifully Wrapped

"It isn't that American women are physically different or deficient. They either don't know it can be done so they don't try, or they are in an environment which is unsupportive, even hostile, and they become discouraged early."
— **Dana Raphael, *The Tender Gift***

Human nutrition via the breast is a huge part of the bonding process. Warm, sweet milk accompanied by warm, soft skin and tender eye contact is a fine recipe for feeling connected to one another.

In a culture where bottle-feeding is the norm, aspiring primal mothers must seek out both education and support. Even though nursing our young is a primal act, part of the process to pass down biological information involves an observation of the experience to which the species is formatted.

La Leche League International is a breastfeeding support organization that educates mothers on the dynamics of breast-feeding and offers ongoing support through family-oriented meetings, literature, telephone consultation, and international conferences. Because of this organization, a helpful breastfeeding mother is never more than a phone call away, night or day. Whether discussing simple breastfeeding techniques, tandem nursing, or even learning to breastfeed an adopted baby, the answers can be found through this valuable group of dedicated lactating women.

When you think about it, no subject on mothering could be more important than breastfeeding. We're talking about the fountain of life, the natural flow of a perfect food which meets the overall needs of our young. From birth right up until the day they bite into a banana and beyond, our babies are assured of everything their little growing bodies need. But, without support from other successful breastfeeding women, we are left exposed and vulnerable to all the breastfeeding-failure horror stories so many women experience, not to mention the formula industry's multi-billion dollar marketing scheme to get our babies latched onto their meal instead of ours.

In the book **Unassisted Childbirth**, Laura Kaplan Shanley discusses the sad consequences of her initial ignorance regarding breastfeeding. Her firstborn was not latching on properly, thus was not able to activate Laura's milk supply to the extent that "hind milk," or the heavier and more nutritious milk which comes toward the end of each feeding would come in. When visited by a social worker just five days after the home birth of her son, rather than informing Laura her baby needed to be taking in more of her nipple for proper sucking and better milk letdown, she instead jotted down a note on her pad of paper, then left. She returned several hours later accompanied by a physician and three policemen, informing Laura they were taking her baby because, according to the social worker, he was too thin and needed to be in a hospital for examining.

It took five horrifying days and nights to get her newborn back into her arms, a nightmare which could have easily been avoided had the social worker chosen to respect the mother/infant bond enough to educate Laura at the moment the problem was apparent. Once the correct nursing process was brought to Laura's attention it was simple to re-position the baby so he was taking in the entire nipple and sucking properly. Like Jonathan Livingston Seagull would say, "It always works when you know what you're doing."

I have been breastfeeding for nearly twelve years now, and I owe my success to my initial commitment in primal mothering, along with female support and personal affirmations. In the beginning I attended monthly La Leche League meetings in my community and developed life-long friendships with the members. I also grabbed hold of the empowering tool known as creative visualization. I taped a beautiful picture of a woman nursing her newborn to my mirror where it reminded me daily of the breastfeeding "reality." I envisioned myself meeting all the nutritional needs of my upcoming child. Contrary to the advice from many around me, I did not buy bottles just in case my milk wouldn't come in. I scruffed up my nipples with a coarse washcloth at shower times to prepare myself for the discomfort that recipients of horror stories insisted I would know. I even shopped the thrift stores for a post-natal wardrobe that would allow easy-access nursing in all situations.

Given the fact my first birthing experience was a medical nightmare, were it not for all my prenatal efforts at creating a successful breastfeeding relationship, I know I would have left the hospital with formula in hand and failure in my heart. Between the breastfeeding ignorance of hospital staff and the formula industry's free-flowing disbursement of their wares (for the specific purpose of getting us, as consumers, hooked on their brand), a mother in the hopes of breastfeeding hardly stands a chance.

Most of the women I talked to who were unsuccessful in their breastfeeding attempts were of the generation when hospitals adhered strictly to four-hour feeding schedules, separating newborns from their mothers upon birth, and bottle-feeding them in the nursery between visits to the mother.

This separation between mother and baby would set the tone for breastfeeding failure. The distress from crying for their mothers and feeling starved on all levels brought these babies to exhaustion, while the stress felt by their mothers, who wondered what was wrong with this picture, inhibited the let-down reflex; thus the doctor's diagnosis that this woman was simply incapable of producing milk.

A newborn is hungry and/or in need of oral gratification for the purposes of security much more often than every four hours, and the hunger pains of an infant are far more intense than those experienced by adults; a physical discomfort which further contributes to the distress which leads to exhaustion. Sucking on a human nipple requires greater physical effort than does sucking on a rubber nipple, so these exhausted and traumatized babies were placated with bottles of sugar water and other horrid concoctions and, therefore, were vulnerable to "nipple confusion" when finally put to their mother's breast.

When these confused little beginners at life finally made it to their mother's breast and sucked with the same ease which brought immediate results from the rubber nipple back at the nursery, nothing would come forth. They gave up and began to cry again. Such a stressful response to nursing then caused their mother to feel inadequate. An added problem to this scenario was the fact that whatever medication was given to their mother during labor and at the time of birth also affected the newborn's initial breastfeeding attempts. With these factors at play, the typical result was a diagnosis of breastfeeding failure and a future of bottle-feeding and formula.

Baby-led breastfeeding, sometimes referred to as on-demand nursing, is the recipe for primal mothering. We intuitively know when our babies are hungry and they intuitively root when they feel hunger, as well as at times when they need reassurance. Why would the female human be the only animal incapable of reading the hunger needs of her young? These last few generations of feeding schedules have contributed greatly to the epidemic eating disorders of our time. Between the crime of being separated from their mother matrix upon birth and the neglect of being denied food when they were hungry in their first hours and days of life (even longer for those babies whose mothers held steady to the doctor's strict feeding plan) is it any surprise we now host the largest eating disordered population anywhere in the world?

As I've shown in the example of a mother who is trying to nurse in the inhospitable conditions of a hospital, stress is generally the major factor involved with any type of breastfeeding complication. I remember my first and only experience with what La Leche League refers to as a nursing strike. My air-conditioner had broken down on a 115 degree Oklahoma summer day, final exams were the following morning, I had a paper due by the next day, and I ended up having to stay at a hotel for the night so as to beat the heat, type up my paper, and finish studying. With all the stress my milk wasn't flowing as usual, and little Sarah Lee was getting frustrated, refusing to keep trying since she couldn't get anywhere in the first place.

It was such a helpless feeling for both of us. I paced the floor all night, holding my hungry, crying baby. I finally made a late-night call to one of my La Leche League friends. She assured me Sarah Lee would not starve to death in the course of a night, and that my "let down" was probably being affected by all the stress I was feeling at the time. I gave up on any ideas of getting sleep that night. Instead, I put her in the sling and walked back and forth while reading my notes and then typed standing up, swaying back and forth as she slept blissfully against me. Come morning, with academic responsibilities behind me, my milk flow resumed and little nurser Sarah Lee made up for lost time.

Modern daily life has enough stress to contend with. We certainly don't need the added strain of societal non-support, but it's a reality which demands our attention. We must prepare ourselves for social pressure. Personal fears about breastfeeding, a partner's embarrassment or insecurity, our family's disapproval, friends' discomfort when with us as we nurse our young, or the professionals and their expert ignorance...at every turn we are faced with advocates for compromise. Like the first time I nursed in public.

My then-husband and I went to a college basketball game. As I settled into my chair, four-day-old Sarah Lee began to root. I automatically lifted my shirt. Immediately my unsupportive spouse turned red from embarrassment and whispered to me, "You're not going to do that HERE!" Just as I was preparing to defend my newborn against his attack a campus policeman came over and asked me to "Please refrain from nursing in this public place." I looked them both square in the eyes and, as if looks could kill, they each backed down and left me alone to feed my hungry newborn.

I am seriously repulsed by men who are not supportive of breastfeeding. Many of these non-supporters condone "closet cases," but they are highly offended when exposed to this nat-ural act in a public place. I once saw a television show where one of the male characters, repulsed by the sight of a mother nursing in a hospital waiting room turned to his friend and said, "Oh, how disgusting! Does she have to do that here?"

That's not funny. That's sick. That's a blatant attack on the innate rights of our children! I'm especially sensitive to this subject of male response to breastfeeding because I spent ten years of my life as a topless dancer, paying my rent with the money tossed to me by men who were enthralled by the sight of bare breasts.

The human female breast has been stolen from its rightful recipients and turned into a sexual object. The American mam-mary glands are literally owned by a breastfeeding-starved adult society comprised of an unsupportive public, a multi-bil-lion-dollar pornography empire, and experts on subliminal mar-keting. It's not just Playboy capitalizing on this cultural hunger. Even women respond sexually to the "public relations" display of breasts. Just try to find an issue of Cosmopolitan WITHOUT the tantalizing effects of cleavage!

There is a particular perversion which occurs in societies

where breastfeeding is no longer the norm. Somehow, the absence of sensual feedings that were biologically expected early on register as a sexual hunger later in life. It's a breast-starved population. Pornography is the prolific weed which inevitably grows in a garden of bottle-fed seedlings.

In our culture, where sexuality and shame are so closely linked, there's a double whammy which makes public breast-feeding even more difficult. As you would have guessed, the basketball game wasn't my last encounter with social resistance to public nursing. In college, male students complained about Sarah Lee nursing while I was in class. In town, restaurant workers glared with disdain as I fed my baby while I tried to enjoy their luncheon special. No better example of the displaced breast could be had than my experience at a nudist community when Sarah Lee was just a toddler. Early one morning, while dangling my legs in the swimming pool, Sarah Lee sat in my lap and quietly began to nurse. Later that day the manager took me aside to say some of their important clientele (all male) had complained about the breastfeeding incident, and for me to refrain from nursing by the pool. By nightfall we were miles down the road, setting our sights on a more supportive environment.

It is true that much of the social disapproval I have endured could have been alleviated by the implementation of a nursing shawl. However, as a primal mother and social reformer, there can be no room in my life for embarrassment, or for acquiescing to social norms. There is no strength in compromise. Not only does an attempt to hide the act of breastfeeding (euphemistically called discreet nursing) exacerbate the already prevalent attitude of shame, but it also denies our babies the wonderful eye contact between mother and child which makes nursing so special. If anything, a shawl strengthens the shame factor, teaching other women — especially girls who are heading into womanhood — that feeding one's baby is an eye-sore to society.

That which is observed on a regular basis is considered normal, which is EXACTLY why social exposure to breastfeeding is so vitally important — despite the glares and other disapproving stares. Public nursing will ultimately create a nursing public. As primal mothers we can't afford to be controlled or silenced by societal disapproval. The bonding process depends on our militant determination to give our children what they need, while we as women exercise our right and responsibility to play an active role in society at large. We cannot bow to this "don't feed your baby in front of me" mentality. I have learned to worry less about whether others are uncomfortable with my public nursing lifestyle, and worry more about being able to comfortably nurse wherever I go. For me, this means wearing a wardrobe which allows for easy access. I have become best friends with the likes of skirts, pareos, shorts, tube tops, halter tops, tank tops, bathing suit tops, and short blouses. At any given moment, no matter what the situation, my children can crawl into my lap and nurse.

Another important consideration is the fact children are born with the desire to play with their food. From the time they are infants, our non-nursing nipple at any given feeding becomes a play-toy. Primal mothers all over the planet have solved this potentially irritating tendency by wearing brightly colored beads around their neck. This delightful diversion entertains the busy little hands of their nurslings. The Affordable Cozy Cradle baby slings I once distributed had a looped ribbon with bright beads securely attached so babies can play with them while nursing.

Slings are wonderful. With our baby right in front of us and so close to our milk supply, we don't have to stop everything we're doing to nourish our young. Once, upon entering a crowded Alcoholics Anonymous meeting, an Indian elder sarcastically shouted to me, "Hey! You're supposed to have your papoose on the back, like they do on my reservation. How come you got that baby in the front?" To his public embarrassment and my primal mothering satisfaction I eloquently replied, "Because my tits are in the front!"

In this day and age, we need a sense of humor to go along with the courage necessary to raise our young straight from the heart. You just never know when yet another "expert" is going to leap out at you.

What little social tolerance there is for breastfeeding quickly dissipates as our infants grow older, especially if that developing infant is a male. It is a sad fact mothers tend to wean their sons much sooner than their daughters. It's a combination of the "You're a big boy now" bullshit and a heavy-duty case of pressure from other family members which kicks our boy babies out of the mothering nest prematurely. My, I wonder if there is any correlation between this breastfeeding fact and the reality that pornography's clientele is primarily male.

Nature would not intend for one gender to be nursed longer than another. ALL children need the breast for as long as it takes to reach satiation in this first and vitally important stage of their overall development. Primal mothers honor child-led weaning. It is not uncommon for a child who is old enough to read and write to need occasional nursing and additional nurturing.

My receptivity to this need in my children has brought me face to face with the Child Protective Services. Neighbors complained I was still nursing Sarah Lee who was then seven years old. Evidently I had mentioned something about it in one of my friendly conversations at the pool-side. A primal mother has the tendency to talk openly about who she is and how she lives her life.

My behavior was being classified as sexual abuse. You've probably heard of various court cases across the country where nursing mothers of young children — as opposed to infants under one year — are being brought to trial for the same reason. I asked the two CPS officers if they were aware of the fact the average duration of breastfeeding worldwide is four years, a statistic which includes nations like ours where we hardly register a duration of six weeks. Therefore, when removing the industrialized nations who have departed from primal mothering practices, the average duration extends to the first seven years of life. They left enlightened, after having closed the case and offered to tell my neighbors to mind their own business.

I had a dream soon after Sarah Lee's birth where I was told she needed to nurse for at least seven years. At the time I had no frame of reference to properly integrate this intuitive message. My La Leche League meetings exposed me to babies as old as two years nursing, but that's as far as my mind could fathom. Then I ran across a magazine where I found a picture showing an eight-year-old boy stopping briefly to nurse at his mothers' breast while she was busy managing her fruit stand at a busy farmer's market in South Africa. I immediately thought back to my dream and realized I was being given confirmation. I asked a few Cherokee elders in my community about their childhood experiences with nursing. Several of them recalled either they themselves or some of their childhood friends to have been nursing occasionally at ages upward of nine and ten.

Weaning is a process that is best accomplished when taking into consideration the emotional needs of our young. And, believe me, nobody else will take those needs into consideration if you don't. The medical profession promotes weaning and the use of a cup long before our children are even one year old. When Sarah Lee was just nine months out of the womb a pediatrician berated me for the fact my child's diet remained exclusively mother's milk. He went on to say I was both irresponsible and unrealistic, that this was not a third world country, and it was my duty to take advantage of all the nutritional advancements America had to offer. Ironic that he was originally from the Orient. People catch on fast to the dysfunctional ways of American society.

We can potentially put our babies' lives at stake when we choose not to nurse, or to wean early. What if there was no formula outlet and you had to rely on your milk supply for hours, days, or weeks on end? Though this scenario may sound far-fetched in our abundant consumerist society, let me give you a couple of examples where breast was not only best but, the only option.

When Sarah Lee was two months old Oklahoma was hit by a devastating twenty-four hour storm and the approach of a tornado. Huddled in the dark and damp tornado shelter for many long hours — with no way of knowing if stores or other formula-dispensing places would be left standing — my infant nursed peacefully. There was virtually no threat to her milk supply. As long as I survived, she would thrive. Seven years later, two-month-old Jasmine at my breast, Hurricane Iniki swept over our tiny Hawaiian island like no hurricane ever had. Whole communities were gathered in public buildings to await the final verdict of this massive storm's rage. Bottle-fed babies cried all through the night and into the morning because their mothers no longer had access to water with which to mix their babies' formula. Only one infant, in a building housing dozens, slept blissfully through that natural catastrophe — little nurser, Jasmine Kokee Halfmoon.

When the hurricane had finally passed and we all set our eyes on what was left of our community, bottle-feeding mothers were faced with the facts. No running water, no way to reach stores which were so badly damaged they were not able to open to the devastated public, starving infants, and empty bottles. These desperate mothers held their screaming babies while watching the skies for military helicopters that were heading our way to drop cases of infant formula.

As much as I wanted to, I could not help those infant victims of hunger. Their relationship to a bottle had clouded over the instinctive memory of a human nipple. They would have literally starved to death before figuring out how to get milk from me. It's scary to see how tenuous is our relationship to primal intellect. We use it or we lose it. What isn't embraced early on appears to be lost for a later time.

We play a potentially deadly game when avoiding the path of primal mothering. How sick, when society is more accepting of the screaming hunger of its newborns than it is of a mother satisfying that newborn's hunger.

Anyone who has ever had a taste of human milk knows the delightfully sweet treat that flows for the sake of humanity. Human milk is composed of water, lactose (sugar), fats (cream) and proteins. The first milk, those few days after our baby is born, is called colostrum. It's a slightly thicker fluid which contains 10% protein, which drops to 2% after only eight days. There is also a high concentration of antibodies immediately after birth which declines rapidly after the first two or three days. Nature inundates the systems of our newborns with exactly what they need to be healthy, and formula industries cannot emulate this vital stage of human feeding.

Sometimes a breastfeeding mother will ask me how she can tell if her baby is getting enough to eat. The proof is in the diaper. Six or more soaked diapers in a twenty-four hour period is ample proof that baby is nursing properly and milk flow is responding to the sucking. For those of you not using the elimination timing method whereby you can see exactly how much your baby is peeing, I highly recommend cloth diapers so you can determine your baby's urinary output. Disposable, plastic diapers absorb the urine in such a way that it is difficult to discern when and how much your baby has eliminated.

Occasionally a newborn will sleep for a very long period of time, not awaken to nurse, thereby hosting a dry diaper. Not to be alarmed. As long as a baby is receiving lots of physical loving attention, especially the kind of attention that is derived from being held in a sling, you don't need to worry about their lengthy slumber and missed feedings. They will wake up when they get hungry enough. As I said before, their hunger pains are strong signals for survival.

As far as bowel movements are concerned, because human milk is so fine-tuned to meet the overall needs of our young, there is little residue that their bodies must push out. Therefore, breastfed babies have fewer and smaller bowel movements than their bottle-fed counterparts. I also want to mention the fact that, as the newborn baby begins life and the necessary process of bowel elimination, their first bowel movement is usually of a tar, almost black color and somewhat mucus-like in texture.

Another concern I hear on a regular basis is whether or not a mother's milk supply will continue for the weeks and months to follow. Breastmilk availability is based on demand and supply; the more demand, the greater the supply. This truth reinforces the warning to steer away from pacifiers and supplemental bottle feedings because the less our babies are sucking on OUR nipples, the less demand on our milk production abilities and the less milk overall. Child-led or on-demand nursing assures us of keeping a quality milk supply. I'm a perfect example of this natural milk-producing phenomenon. My milk has been flowing steadily for over a decade. And no, I don't consume huge amounts of dairy products to keep up this lactating momentum. In fact, I don't touch animal products at all. My diet is comprised primarily of fruit with some vegetables, nuts, and seeds.

Putting children other than our own to our breasts is another misunderstood primal reality, one our society neither acknowledges nor seems to remember from its recent past. A primal mother doesn't deny a hungry infant her breasts, whether that child is her biological offspring or not. There is something very ancient and sacred about serving the needs of children in our midst. This primal sense of responsibility develops in our offspring a deep sense of trust in women, knowing that mothers in general care deeply about the particular needs of any child.

I have nursed any child who needed comfort and/or food and find it strange people can get into such an uproar over nursing someone else's young — have they never heard the term "wet nurse?" Many of our recent ancestors had wet nurses during their infancy and beyond. Keep in mind the bottle is a recent invention compared to the long history of the delightfully beautiful female breast and its sweet flowing milk. If I was a baby I'd much prefer enveloping my searching mouth around the soft nipple of a loving woman than stare at an upright plastic bottle.

For those of you who don't like visits to the doctor or dentist, breastfeeding is the way to go. The more aggressive style of sucking necessary for breastfed babies results in greater jaw development and thus better spacing for teeth. Babies who are breastfed for at least six months have three times fewer ear infections than babies who are not given mother's milk; five times fewer urinary tract infections; five times fewer serious illnesses; and seven times fewer allergic reactions. And babies fed from the milk of fruitarian mothers enjoy an infancy devoid of any physical ailments.

Women who breastfeed for a lifetime total of two years have forty percent less incidence of breast cancer. Women who have been breastfed as infants have a twenty-six percent less breast cancer incidence than women who were not breastfed.

Breastfeeding also delays the return of fertility. Breastfed children are less likely to develop diabetes. Breastfeeding enhances intellectual development. Prolonged lactation results in greater weight loss for the mother from one to twelve months postpartum. Human milk lessens the risk of diarrhea for the breastfeeding baby. Breastfeeding promotes dental health. Breastmilk has antibacterial properties. Breastfeeding greatly reduces the threat of Sudden Infant Death Syndrome. Colostrum, the first milk, is a complete food for the newborn. Diaper rash occurs less, and diaper duty itself is more pleasant because the odor from the feces of a breastfed baby is sweet compared to the foul smell derived from formula or other non-human milk.

Human milk meets human needs. Formula is a dismal imitator, and cow's milk is designed to build cows, not humans. The survival organ of cows is their muscles for the purpose of running from predators, thus their milk is specifically tuned to building massive muscle. That explains why a calf gains some four pounds daily thereby quickly attaining its large mass. By comparison, the survival organ of our human species is the brain, and human milk specifically feeds brain development. Mother's milk literally feeds the intellect of humanity.

This nutritional axiom sheds a brilliant light on the fact that, in just a few generations, we have managed to decimate the planet and its diverse inhabitants. It is these same few generations who have, for the most part, been denied nature's brain food.

Our culture has a highly illusory relationship to cow's milk in particular and animal products in general. The osteoporosis scare is just one of many hypes used to convince people of their "need" for these foods. Why, then, in the country where the largest consumption of animal products occurs we find the highest rate of osteoporosis? The truth of the matter is we are consuming far too much of the wrong kinds of calcium and protein, thus poisoning ourselves in an effort to ingest what authorities tell us we need. Let's not forget that the nutritional authorities are politically and financially related to the unbelievably high profits derived from the sale of animal products, and other foods such as cereals that are always accompanied by milk.

We can clearly see the ridiculousness of adopting cow's milk into the diet of our children. With our minds back in our possession, let's get on to the subject of nature's bridge from breastmilk to bananas. Just how long does breastmilk meet the growing needs of our young, and what happens next?

My children were exclusively breastfed for the first year, and more than ninety percent of their diet continued to come from my milk into and even past their second year, with the introduction of such fruits as watermelon, bananas, coconut, papayas, and avocados.

Transitioning from human milk to the next step in the human dietary is host to yet another barrage of social myths and other nutritional assumptions. Judging by my own experience and the perfect health of my children, fruit is nature's plan for the next phase of culinary delight. After all, a freshly picked fig or mango — according to all the senses — is as pleasing as one's experience at the breast.

Being the die-hard detective of human roots that I am, my search for nature's nutritional plan unfolded this knowledge to me as gracefully and penetratingly as had those insights about birthing, bonding, and breastfeeding. I was reading an article about primates when the proverbial light went on in my head.

The author was describing how baby primates naturally transition from mother's milk to fruit and that, in fact, the nutritional composition of primate milk is nearly identical to that of fruit.

Chapter 6

FRUITARIAN MOTHERING
Paradise Found

*"The plant-eaters still form at the present time,
as they have always done, the great majority of animals
on earth. The most highly developed plant eaters are
fruit eaters; the highest fruit eater is the human being."*
— **Dr. O.L.M. Abramowski**
Fruitarian Diet and Physical Rejuvenation

There is a vibration in the word "fruitarian" which taps into our primal core, our innate knowledge of nutrition. It's the Garden of Eden erected within. Every mother can relate to the wonderful sense of responsibility she feels when offering her children fruit. It's the same awesome sense of responsibility, combined with serenity and calm, which accompanies the act of breastfeeding.

In fact, perfectly ripe fruit IS mother's milk. When our own diet consists primarily of fruit, we can count on a healthy production of rich milk in all necessary constituents for meeting the needs of our young. As stated in the last chapter, primate babies go straight from their mother's milk to succulent fruit. And so it can be with our own growing babies.

Our children love and thrive on fruit, easily assimilating all of the amino acids (protein), calories, carbohydrates, essential vitamins, fat, calcium and other minerals necessary to develop and maintain the powerfully strong and agile frames which keep them playing hard from sun-up to sun-down, day in and day out.

Fruit is a cleansing food that delivers necessary nutrients in correct proportions to all the cells of our bodies. Fruit digests easily due to its highly usable constituents, and supplies our bodies with a high level of water which further keeps our systems from experiencing constipation.

Unlike the poor combinations derived from animal products and other processed foods, fresh fruits enter our mouth in all their deliciousness and activate the enzymes necessary for quick digestion. With fruit, the stomach serves as a corridor whereas, when consuming the Standard American Diet (SAD), the stomach becomes a holding tank for putrefaction and fermentation. We don't have to be SAD, we can LAF (eat Live Alkaline Fruits) and experience the true joy of life!

The antacid industry would fold up within the month if our population embraced fruit as a dietary focus. Why? Because the poor combinations of already poor food choices creates an acidic environment in the stomach which results in chronic indigestion. The multi-billion-dollar success of the antacid industry relies heavily on this combination of events.

In contrast, fruit is alkaline upon digestion and therefore matches the body's natural alkaline state. Human milk also reflects the alkaline balance of our human physiology, whereas cow's milk and other formulas are acidic. Understanding the composition of breastmilk can lead us to insights about necessary dietary needs for the weaned and beyond. Human milk is a low protein, high fat, and very sweet food packed full of all the nutrients necessary for newborns to double their weight in a matter of months. Since the amount of protein we need lessens slightly after the first months of life, and the ratio of amino acids (pre-digested protein) in fruit is just slightly lower than that of breastmilk, the nutritional composition of fruits responsibly carries on the role of growing our baby's bodies and maintaining their health.

When my mothering career began twelve years ago I started transitioning to a fruitarian diet. As a result of this alignment to nature's plan my children have enjoyed superb health, and I have levels of physical and mental energy beyond measure. My emotional attachments to cooked and other junk foods have been challenged at every turn, but the reward of improved health has always kept me going in the right direction. My book **Cooked Foods Anonymous** is dedicated to addressing this issue of cooked-food dependency and offers a recovery program that is realistic, revealing, and produces fantastic results.

Finding our roots in fruitarianism requires the courage to address our emotional attachment to many culturally acceptable food choices. And sometimes that courage gets stretched to the point of confronting "authority" figures who cannot see beyond the cultural norm. I once had neighbors who called the Child Protective Services on me because my children were not receiving the kinds of foods they deemed normal and necessary. That night a police officer came to my door saying there was a complaint of neglect. He said he needed to look into my cupboards to see if I had any food. Having just shopped at the health food store that afternoon, I was looking forward to educating this obese uniformed officer. Upon opening first one cupboard and then the next, he turned to me with a surprised look on his face and said, "Hey, you don't have ANY food in your house!"

I suggested he look down at the table he was leaning over. His strained leather belt responsible for holding in his huge pot-belly was bruising my food supply — a table heavy-laden with more than fifty pounds of fresh, organic fruit; watermelon, oranges, papayas, pineapple, bananas, apples, and figs. I motioned him to the refrigerator where awaited shelves of fresh organic vegetables. And then I finished this tour by pointing to the two five-pound glass jars of nuts and dried fruits on my kitchen counter. His reply, "But you don't have any milk or canned goods. I'm going to have to fill out a report and you will be hearing from the Child Protective Services over the next few days."

I called them rather than waiting to receive their call. After complaining about this intrusion by the ignorant officer, I took the time to educate this woman about fruitarianism. By the time our conversation was coming to a close she admitted, "I can't really argue with you. After all, your children have never been sick a day in their lives. In fact, in many ways I admire you for having the courage to live up to what you know is right. I will close this case because there is no substantial evidence of neglect."

We literally have to fight for what is natural. Just today I received a letter from a reader who was livid over the fact that a recent radio show was discussing whether it should be legal for women to breastfeed in public. It is clearly time to change this trend of thought. Baring the human breast is beautiful; raping beasts for their milk is sinister. Feeding our children from the fruit of the earth is divine; killing animals for their meat is a serious fault.

I won't even jump in the debating ring when it comes to the subject of consuming animal "products." My simple response to the claim humans are naturally meat-eaters is this...fruit will rot if not appreciated in its ripened state, whereas an animal will continue to enjoy life, mate, raise babies, cuddle with their young, play, and otherwise prosper in life if left to their own true destiny.

Nothing is destroying our planetary resources and the health of humanity faster than the consumption and exploitation of animals. The sooner we acknowledge and respond to both animal rights and human health needs, the sooner we can begin the healing process that will send us in a direction honoring the seventh generation from now. When one woman stops buying animal "products," that's one less consumer for the meat and dairy industry and one less ill individual for the animal experimentation (vivisection) industry to exploit with medicine. When that same woman fills her grocery basket with fresh, organic fruits and vegetables, that's a vote in the direction of stronger orchards and gardens — a powerful vote that pulls us closer to Paradise.

I often hear mothers insist they cannot afford to feed their family in this way, that the cost of fresh fruits and vegetables is simply beyond their budget. Eating right only stretches the budget when the unhealthy foods remain in the picture. Across the board, it costs less to eat healthfully. I spend approximately $100 per week to feed my family of four. With this money, I bring home seventy pounds of bananas, twenty pounds of oranges, ten pounds of apples, twenty pounds of melon, two pounds of almonds, twenty pounds of papaya, three heads of lettuce, two pounds of carrots, ten pounds of avocados, and three pineapples. Most of this food is organic, and I'm talking about Hawaii prices! So you can imagine just how financially palatable the Paradise Diet can be in other regions of the world where prices are undoubtedly less than what I am paying.

We love to start our first meal of the day with watermelon in the hot tub. It's a warm, sweet, and cozy way to connect with one another before venturing off into our individual realities in the security and comfort of home. The rest of the morning is replete with fresh fruit juices and frozen banana smoothies, adding whatever fruit sounds fun at the time. I also fill plastic popsicle holders with the smoothie mixture so that my children and their friends can enjoy healthy treats throughout the day.

In the afternoon I make large fruit or vegetable platters and my children grab from it whenever hunger strikes. I arrange these fruit or vegetable pieces atop lettuce leaves, and we roll up our produce burrito-style. Children love to participate in food preparation. For the fruitarian child, meal-time is "arts & crafts" time!

My dear fruitarian-friend Jennifer Vanlaanen-Smit, whose natural beauty graces the front cover of this book, has shared one of her children's very favorite recipes with us....a primal rendition of the peanut-butter & jelly sandwich!

1. To make fresh nutbutter, soak almonds overnight. Rinse and put through a food processor.

2. To make fresh jam, soak dehydrated fruit overnight. Drain (her kids love drinking the juice!) and put through blender or food processor. Keep in refrigerator.

3. Slice bananas in half lengthwise. Spread jam on one side, nutbutter on the other, place raisins along the top and then stack one banana slice on top of the other.

4. Wrap the stuffed banana in a lettuce leaf.

When I met Jennifer nearly three years ago she was intrigued by the fact that my family practiced fruitarianism. It made so much sense to her primal mothering instincts she immediately began transitioning her family from a vegan diet to one consisting primarily of fruit. She is astounded at the many wonderful benefits which have come from this transition to fruitarianism and she fully admits the difficulties she has faced along the way...

"I cannot believe how hard it is to stop wanting potatoes. This has been my hardest food to quit. It is my comfort food and makes me feel warm inside. This was my last step to an all-raw diet...those damn potatoes call to me. Well, I did it. No more potatoes or cooked food for me! This is how I got to my all-raw diet. First I realized that with the cooked foods I was craving, I was only craving the sauce and spices, not the pasta, potatoes, or rice itself. I decided to 'let' myself eat the cooked 'dead' item, but only in a salad (I mean mixed into the salad) and then I gradually put less and less of the starchy cooked stuff into my living salads. I also made up a raw sauce similar to what I liked and made up a raw veggie equivalent to my cooked craving...raw veggie burgers, carrot/beet/zucchini/sprout pasta, veggie tacos, raw falafels, raw sandwich middles stuffed in a lettuce leaf, raw pies, cakes, cookies, breads, raw pizza, etc. This has let me have

my comfort foods, keep my raw diet, and be healthy too! My
kids have had an easier time with these familiar 'tastes' and eat
more without me coercing them to. When I go into the health
food store and I go past the hot-food bar, I still stop and think
about picking up some sauteed potatoes or spaghetti, but the
thought lasts about thirty seconds as I pass by. If I am hungry, I
grab some fruit — a banana, peach, grapes and eat that as soon
as I buy them. This tastes much better than any dead food I
could have, and I feel good about my choice. This works with
my kids also; I buy the fruit before I shop for other items and
they munch the sun's sweet treats as we pass by cookies, the
hot-food bar, breads, etc. Also, another thing I do to keep raw is
I avoid the rest of the store and head straight to the produce isle
and then to the cashier. If I do end up buying a cooked
processed food I will either eat it or throw it away — both are
not good so I just don't buy it. I always bring with us on any car
trip a bunch of bananas, grapes, apple slices, etc. so if my kids
even think about getting hungry, they have something quick and
easy. The farmer's market is fun and you don't pass by the
cookie/snack, hot dog, ice cream isles on the way to the tomatoes." Jennifer and I have co-authored the book **Raw Food
Recipes: A Fruitarian Child's Delight!** which is available
through Nature's First Law at 1-800-205-2350.

The intensity of transition varies from person to person.
While some women find it relatively easy to act on their newly
re-discovered knowledge of natural nutrition, others, myself
included, struggle with an emotional attachment to heavier,
cooked foods. The following letter is testimony to this struggle:

"It has been over a year since Hygeia first introduced me to
fruitarianism. I am still working on it. It's not the concept I have
trouble with. I fully believe in the abundant physical, mental,
and spiritual benefits that fruitarianism offers. It's not external
forces I'm having trouble with. I've been able to toss them off
for some time, considering the many nonconformist decisions
I've made in my life. It's addiction. I have an addiction to

cooked food. It's a helpless feeling that I despise, but there's no denying it. I often feel out of control when it comes to eating. But I feel that fruitarianism has opened my eyes. I now know that I don't need ANY of the foods that trigger the addiction in me. I've never had a fruit binge. I am strictly an emotional eater. Anger, loneliness, boredom, guilt; they are all key emotions that can bring on a bout of binge eating. It may seem to the critics in my life that I have not made any progress in the past year. Indeed, in times of self doubt, I tell myself that very thing. But now I can WITNESS MY BEHAVIOR. Before I took a serious look at my eating habits with a true knowledge of my physiological needs at hand, I ate large amounts of SAD (Standard American Diet) food, sometimes going days or weeks without any living food. Now I KNOW that sort of eating is energy-draining and does not nurture my whole self. I still have many days I feel I haven't tried at all, but I AM conscious of the mistakes I make and the repercussions they have on my life. I can no longer be ignorant (much as my addiction wishes I were) and ask myself, 'Why am I so fat?' or 'Why am I so sick?' or 'Why don't I have any energy?' I KNOW the reason. I am responsible for the way I feel. Along with the wonderful, life-giving aspects of fruit, it is the self-discipline that it takes to say NO to my addiction and hold on for a more pure and righteous high that makes fruitarianism a complete journey to health."

In these years of working with other aspiring fruitarians, I have noticed that the single most difficult food for most people to let go of is pizza. I can attest to this addiction because my own experience with Italian buffets kept me going back for more of the same. T.C. Fry once told me that the chemical combinations derived from the cheese, wheat, cooked tomatoes, and spices create an effect similar to ingesting marijuana. Yes, I'll be the first to admit that I got high eating pizza and, oh, what a crash when detoxification time rolled around!

Fouad "Raw Courage" Dini, co-author of **Nature's First**

Law: The Raw-Food Diet, offers a most insightful allegory on the true nature of pizza...

"By letting go of pizza you'll become stronger and stronger in every way until the day comes when you look down and see pizza for what it truly is. With instinctual clarity the pizza will zoom in on you, making you dizzy with the same fear that makes you dizzy when you look down into the depths of a precipice. Panic resembling vertigo will overwhelm your senses and self-preserving warning signals will flare within you. Your eyes will focus on the pizza the same way they focus down the depths of the fall. Your mind will recognize the danger both pizza and plunge bring, and will react to them as the equal threats they are. Looking down, your Life Force will focus into the depths of despair pizza brings and will see its death. In a calm fright your mind will freeze and your body will clench with the same involuntary instincts that forbid you from stepping off a cliff."

If you find yourself in this category, struggling to free yourself from unhealthy food choices, please nurture yourself with my book **Cooked Foods Anonymous**. With the help of this book specifically designed to assist the transition process, the day will soon come when there will be ample support for the aspiring fruitarian, when we will find a CFA (Cooked Foods Anonymous) meeting right in our own communities on any given day.

A great first step toward fruitarianism is to serve your family fruit only until noon. Make fresh fruit juices, banana smoothies, fruit salads, whatever sounds fun. Every morning my children and I enjoy a fruit meal in the hot tub. We discuss our dreams of the night before, or give gratitude for upcoming events, all the while watermelon juice is running down our arms. Mornings are such a precious time anyway, which makes incorporating the Paradise diet that much easier.

As time goes on, extend your fruit meals beyond noon. From there, offer your family a beautifully arranged vegetable platter with avocado dip. As evening approaches, minimize the consumption of cooked food by first serving a huge salad, and then a plentiful supply of slightly-steamed vegetables. Or, better yet, try Jennifer's suggestion of combining the cooked food right into a huge, luscious living salad. The key to success is "massive raw foods action." In time, the rest will take care of itself.

It is only fitting to end this chapter with a momentous event which took place in my home a few days ago. While sitting on the floor with my family and enjoying the sweet, buttery taste of avocados that my twelve-year-old daughter Sarah Lee had climbed at great height to pick for our family just days prior, she smiled in satisfaction and said, "I'm glad we eat the way we do, so we can appreciate what we eat."

Chapter 7

NATURAL HYGIENE
Human Intelligence At Its Finest

*"The operations of cooking and refining are not only
unnatural, harmful, and break the Laws of Nature,
but they are the primary cause of all disease."*
— **Arlin / Dini / Wolfe**, *Nature's First Law:
The Raw-Food Diet*

The basic foundation of natural hygiene is that the body is always striving for health and it achieves this by continuously cleansing itself of deleterious waste material.

This explains why the best foods for both nurturing and cleansing the body are raw fruits. These high-water content, vitamin-rich, mineral-laden meals pick up where breastmilk leaves off when it comes to feeding the body's cells, including those more than twenty five million brain cells which make up our specie's survival organ.

Simply put, we think and function better when partaking of such a hygienic food as delicious fruit. With nature's correct diet, our brains receive everything necessary to maintain this complex intelligence site that is one of the most highly developed among any species.

It is our brains that make our decisions, and a clear-headed human makes for better decision-making. A primal mother doesn't accept the advice and opinions of others but rather, she looks deeply into everything that caresses her primal intellect while questioning anything that does not resonate with her soul. I love what Marilyn and Harvey Diamond say in their brilliant best-seller **Fit For Life**, "It is time to take control and responsibility back from those who are arguing about who has the right answer."

Speaking of looking for the right answers, since a discussion about the true roots of human nutrition generally leads to a battle of beliefs between evolutionists and creationists, allow me to share this simple yet profound story:

A conference took place where both creationists and evolutionists gathered to argue their beliefs. One at a time, they took to the podium and espoused what they each insisted were absolute truths. Finally an old Indian woman got up from her seat and slowly approached the podium. Taking the microphone into her hand she looked out over the audience and calmly reported, "The earth rests on the back of a turtle." She removed her hand from the mouth-piece and started back to her seat. The audience began to snicker. One of the experts called out, "Excuse me, but what is the turtle resting on?" Everyone started laughing until she responded, "Why, the back of another turtle, of course." Anticipating the next question she added, "Don't bother asking. It's turtles all the way down."

This story reflects a great truth...one creation story is just as good (humorous, ridiculous, incredulous, etc.) as another. Nature's First Law distributes a booklet entitled: **On Form And Actuality** which provides great insight into this subject. The wide range of beliefs concerning our human dietary heritage creates a similar argument between experts while the masses obediently wait for the test results to hit the press — after the laboratory rat has lived or died — thereby learning what the latest dietary requirements are and what we supposedly need for optimum health.

Optimum health? Obviously these experts are not on the right track. According to the United States Surgeon General, of the

2.1 million Americans who die each year, 1.5 million, 68%, die from diet-related disease...specifically heart-disease, cancer, and stroke. Still, people prefer to believe they are hit by a disease rather than assume responsibility for their condition of ill health. Even the doctors on whom society depends cannot save themselves from the consequences of the standard american diet (SAD). As reported by Laura Kaplan Shanley in her masterpiece **Unassisted Childbirth**, "Physicians have an intellectual understanding of the process of digestion, yet it doesn't prevent them from having one of the highest ulcer rates of any profession." In fact, the leading prescription drug in this country is for stomach disorders, and a large percentage of our population actually needs assistance from a laxative to have a bowel movement!

Society has such an obsession with food and with using the mouth as an entertainment device there seems to be widespread denial when it comes to acknowledging any correlation between what we eat and our level of health. Our epidemic rates of eating disorders which lead to obesity, malnourishment, and every other disease you can imagine parallels the fact our culture represents a few generations of non-breastfed people. Perhaps a lack of satiation at the breast during infancy and early childhood leaves the adult human grappling chronically and hopelessly to satisfy an oral need. This, on top of eating foods which are not only devoid of the nutritional elements found in fruit but also brimming with toxicity, creates a sick society.

Denial dies hard. Most people still prefer to believe they have been "bit by the bug" rather than accept the stronger probability that it was what they bit into that caused their health problems in the first place. Computer language calls it the GI-GO factor....garbage in, garbage out. What we eat does affect every aspect of our health.

Disease is what we feel when the body is in the process of healing itself. Healing is the process of neutralizing and eliminating accumulated toxins and repairing damaged structures and cells. And the symptoms represent our body's intelligent avenues for removing those toxins from our systems.

Natural hygiene is a nutritional science which places health responsibility squarely on the shoulders of each and every adult who, in turn, become role models to the children in their lives. Natural hygiene blasts away at our complacency, our personal lethargy that leads us around as if we are tethered to the latest nutritional theory discharged by the food and drug administration. Thinking for ourselves and believing in our choices is the mark of a sovereign soul. To become a "Siddhartha" in our own lives is the greatest gift we can give to ourselves, and a most necessary role-model of self-sufficiency for our children.

Like primal mothering, natural hygiene is not something we learn but rather, it is something we remember. The information lives inside our cells. Human beings are perfect self-healing organisms. All of the wisdom and instructions for self-healing are encoded in our genes. True knowledge is available not only to the literate; true knowledge resides within our very being.

The dismissal of social beliefs within the context of our own minds is a challenge that we must take on. This exorcism of social thought demands confidence in ourselves, a characteristic seldom developed when we have spent most of our lives listening to and believing in the messages rendered by the patriarchal likes of politicians, popes, physicians, and pharmaceutical giants. It takes perseverance to break past these barriers which have been designed to keep us at bay from our primal intellect. All the self-doubt that arises, all the criticism we face, it's enough to make any truth-seeker frustrated and in jeopardy of giving up.

J.H. Tilden, MD, a pioneer in the field of natural hygiene reflects in his book **Toxemia Explained**, "When I think back over my life, and remember the struggle I had with myself in supplanting my old beliefs with the new — the thousands of times I have suspected my own sanity — I then cannot be surprised at the opposition I have met and am meeting."

Awakening to the knowledge of human nutrition and having the will power to activate that knowledge can be two different things. My early years of midnight bingeing on white bread began a lifetime eating disorder for me. I have always relied on food for emotional comfort, especially heavy, starchy foods like breads, pastas, pizza, cereals, and high-fat sweets. I receive letters all the time from people who find these same foods to be their downfall. One man wrote, "I wouldn't be surprised if cooked starches, being slower to digest and quicker to spoil, create some alcohol in the system, leading to a mild form of alcoholism. They affect me like a drug — I'm extremely addicted to them and they bring my health down tremendously."

I refer to the chemical response derived from cooked starches as endogenous alcoholism. It wasn't until I could let go of cooked starch that my journey into health really began.

When I awoke to my fruitarianism, I was faced with the rebellious power of cooked/processed-food addiction, especially the cooked starches and, most specifically, pasta and pizza. I had to become willing to confront my attachment to these "comfort" foods which took the edge off my life's problems. By adopting the 12-step A.A. program I used for my previous recovery from alcoholism I was able to recognize my powerlessness over these unhealthy foods, unearth my personality insecurities which led to a need for comfort, and then find healthy ways to nurture myself.

This transition was not overnight. After all, my emotional problems had not been built overnight. They represented years of nutritional, spiritual, and sensual neglect. In **Fit For Life** Marilyn and Harvey Diamond gently remind us, "You have certain cravings that you have built up over the years. It's going to take a certain amount of time for you to overcome these cravings."

We cannot simply let go of the very pain which keeps driving us back to numbing foods. Pain is the by-product of something having gone terribly awry, and layers upon layers of subconscious protective mechanisms keep us at bay from the original grief. In truth, we must dive into our pain and trust we will first survive and then eventually thrive as a result of this courageous act in self-disclosure. In the book **The Prophet**, Kahlil Gibran writes "Who can depart from his pain and his aloneness without regret? It is not a garment I cast off this day, but a skin that I tear with my own hands."

It is for this very reason we need a recovery movement that deals specifically with abstention from cooked food. Cooked Foods Anonymous (CFA) will be the support system for this species of ours who has strayed so violently from its roots. My books **Highway To Health: A Call To Fruitarianism** and **Cooked Foods Anonymous** are completely devoted to guiding cooked-food addicts back home to the Garden.

The 12-step programs enjoy a high success rate because they cater to the basal needs of newcomers (newborns, so to speak). The newcomer is immediately accepted for exactly who they are at that exact moment, and for everything they have done in their past. Nothing is being shoved down their throat. The only requirement for membership is a desire to stop eating cooked food (drinking, smoking, or whatever specific addiction that particular program is addressing). The newcomer is constantly reminded they are the most important person in the room. In effect, a CFA meeting creates for the newcomer a place of rebirthing whereby she receives all the love and attention she was denied in her infancy.

One of the most common complaints about Alcoholics Anonymous is the heavy use of coffee and cigarettes at meetings. This sucking and sipping behavior makes perfect sense when you really stop to think about it. The group offers everything BUT the breast, and the breast was designed to come with the territory of unconditional love. Cooked Foods Anonymous meetings will complete the circle. In these warm and friendly groups, the members will be sipping on fresh fruit juices while working the twelve steps of recovery that lead to a personal transformation, making them the happy people they were intended to be — happy, joyous, and free.

Creating the support needed to overcome our dependency on cooked foods catapults us into the benefits of natural truths. Natural hygiene is a science that finds truth in simplicity, and the truth it sheds regarding illness couldn't get more simple.

All disease is narrowed down to one cause — toxicosis. And the cure for said disease is, simply — detoxification. The high-water content and healthy fiber found in fruit helps our bodies to pass waste products out of our systems expediently. When our bodies are inundated with low-water and no-water content foods on a regular basis, a host of events take place which often lead to enervation and an accumulation of toxins in our systems.

The friendly diet of fruit literally cleanses our systems of tox-ins, and brings nutrients in the right amounts to our cells. Traumatic events from the past and other emotional pain which had previously been repressed are often released and swept away in the course of our body's efforts to cleanse.

When we avoid the cleansing benefits of a natural diet and instead feed our children cooked and processed food, they tend to suffer from such maladies as colic, ear infections, asthma, congestion, dental caries, tonsilitis, measles, chicken pox, mumps, and other childhood complications. Those youngsters who do manage to get past childhood without bothersome ill-nesses may be met later in life with the more chronic levels of toxicosis which result in cancer, heart disease, arthritis, etc.

In the case of illness (toxicosis, to be exact), removing toxins from our systems is an easy process that includes a combination of high fruit intake, occasional fasting, and exercise. As a nurs-ing mother, I adopt an occasional fast which involves the use of watermelon juice rather than just water because I need to main-tain my milk supply. Detoxification symptoms often include physical exhaustion, coated tongue, foul breath, body odor, fever, elimination of mucus, loose stools, vomiting, and aching muscles. Since my milk supply reflects the busy elimination process going on in my own body, my breastfeeding babies may experience detoxification symptoms right along with me. That's OK. I'd rather share the discomfort of detoxification now than play resident host to future disease for both of us.

Children detoxify beautifully on fruit juices. You've noticed how children lose their appetite when they feel sick. Sips of water or juice are their only request. That's because they are adhering to their primal urge to fast; they are listening to their cellular knowledge, in modern terms referred to as natural hygiene.

While doing my doctoral internship at a fasting retreat in Texas I observed the natural course of detoxification in the cases of several children who were under my care. Rather than encourage a water fast I simply offered them as much juicy fruit (oranges, grapes, watermelon) as they wanted — and no other foods. Within a few days of eating fruit and playing hard, their little bodies began to harness energy for cleansing that had, before they arrived, been used for the digestion of cooked starches, animal products, and processed foods. They lost all interest in eating, slept most of the day and all through the night, and exhibited such detoxification symptoms as fever, nausea, runny nose, diarrhea, and vomiting. After a few days of this intense elimination, they slowly showed interest in sips of freshly-squeezed orange juice and, before long, were back outside jumping and hollering and hanging from tree limbs, calling out for bananas. Their innate intelligence had allowed nature to run its course.

Fasting our babies is a challenge requiring a minute-by-minute review of their stress level. As one breastfeeding mother wrote, "In the midst of my own journey toward fruitarianism, I made an exception by having a piece of cake while at a party. The result of this was that my baby developed a stuffy nose. He was having tremendous trouble nursing because he could not breathe through his nose, so he was not only feeling bad, he was hungry. Rather than have him in the Cozy Cradle where he kept wanting to nurse, I put him in the backpack and went about weeding flowerbeds. When he would get totally cranky, I would take him out and he would eagerly attack a bottle of water. After a few pulls, he would realize it was me giving the bottle, and that it was not his usual delightful milk, and promptly quit sucking. This was usually enough to get him satisfied and asleep, though. I also pushed him around in the stroller in the sun and a great amount of mucus poured from his nose, as well as a good deal of sweating. I was able to keep the fast up for eight hours, until he had reached his tolerance level for the experience, and then began to nurse regularly again. The first nursing was struggle-free, as his nose had really cleared up. He resumed nursing with his usual gusto."

My "falls" from grace have been the reason for any and all of the physical discomforts my breastfeeding babies have ever known. If anything, this sad domino effect sheds further light on the powerlessness we sometimes face when struggling to free ourselves from cooked food. All the more reason to nurture ourselves with the support we need so that we may, in turn, nurture our babies with the healthiest of breastmilk. The friendliest approach to fasting our babies is to nurse them as little as possible for a day or two, wear them constantly, and be physically active enough for the rhythmic motions of our body to keep them sleeping throughout most of the day. Their bodies heal most efficiently when they are asleep. Expose them to plenty of sunshine, and offer sips of water where possible. You will be amazed at how quickly babies respond to fasting. They are proof of our nature to be whole and the body's ability to expediently right the wrongs.

Sunlight helps the body heal wounds and injuries and overcome virtually any illness. Though sunscreen manufacturers rely heavily on a fear-based society, we don't have to buy into the skin cancer scare. Fruitarians have a healthy relationship to the sun because their skin's surface is not playing the role of a griddle to baking toxins. Every part of us needs the nurturing rays of the sun. The highest rates of cancer are in those bodily regions we keep consistently covered: breast, reproductive organs, and colon.

We need to make every effort to sunbathe nude on a regular basis. The improved amounts of vitamin D made by this sun exposure will greatly improve our health and well-being. Simply put, we look better, feel better, get better, and function better after exposing ourselves to the sun's warm rays.

Our eyes need sunshine just as much as the rest of our bodies. Dr. Herbert Shelton reports, "Gazing directly into the sun actually improves sight and aids in overcoming disease." Psychic awareness is also greatly enhanced by drawing our visual attention to the life-giving forces of the sun.

Nature has a health plan for women that in no way reflects the present assault on our mothering organs. Breast cancer and pelvic problems have become an epidemic for the modern female. Because the body intelligently stores toxins in those organs least likely to cause immediate death (as opposed to the heart or brain, for instance), breasts and sexual organs are generally utilized for the temporary storage of toxins.

When we ovulate each month and no pregnancy ensues, the uterus then sloughs off the endometrial lining. The degree of bleeding during this sloughing off period is directly proportional to the accumulation of toxins in this bodily region. It is no secret that vegetarian women bleed less during menses than those who eat animal products, while physically active fruitarian women bleed little or not at all. One aspiring fruitarian mother wrote, "I am AMAZED at how much heavier my menstrual flow was after bingeing so much. And now that I look back, it used to be that way EVERY MONTH!"

When we use our breasts for their biological function, our breasts are not stagnant, and therefore toxins don't get an opportunity to build up. This fact is clearly indicated by studies showing breast cancer to be nearly non-existent among women who breastfeed for up to two years and more. The longer they nurse, the lower the incidence of cancer. A case in point.....

Thirty years ago, my mother who bottle-fed her children wore bandages on her surgically removed once-breast area of her chest to catch the oozing toxins while today I am breastfeeding and wearing folded up bandanas to soak up the over-flowing milk supply of one breast while nursing with the other side. My mother died from toxicosis (breast cancer) at the age of thirty-six. I am enjoying superb health at the age of forty-four...thanks to fruitarianism and over a decade of breastfeeding my young.

We DO have control over our family's health. Diseases don't strike us, they grow inside of us in direct proportion to the types of foods we eat, the emotions we choose to nurture, the amount of exercise we get, the stress levels we experience, the relationships we attract, and the belief systems we embrace. Every day new designer drugs, or interventive medical procedures accompanied by — you guessed it — more new designer drugs arrive on the social scene to further whisk our symptoms under the rug, side-stepping the true issue...the source of our malady.

Drugs interfere with the body; that's why they have side effects. Vaccinations are a perfect example of this reality. For hours and even days after our babies have been stabbed by a stranger in white, they exhibit severe symptoms of detoxification, especially fever and vomiting. The intelligence of their little bodies is trying desperately to remove the foreign and dangerous intruder.

When my first-born Sarah Lee was just two months old, I obediently brought her in for the beginning of her youthful round of immunizations. The moment the intrusive needle went into her leg and a tremendous scream left her lungs I knew that this was wrong. Prior to that moment I claimed ignorance because I didn't understand the reasons behind immunizations and I certainly didn't know I had a choice in the matter. I grabbed her away from the nurse and ran out the door. This horrible experience sent me reeling into research and I soon learned that the vaccination movement is a multi-billion dollar pharmaceutical gold-mine.

By now you must be getting the message that the owners of this lucrative and ludicrous pharmaceutical empire are in all reality the pimps who keep their prostitute physicians filling out those prescription pads and telling mothers what horrible nightmares might happen if they don't follow doctor's orders.

They don't mention the fact that cancer rates among children have skyrocketed since vaccinations have come on the scene, nor do they share the true nightmares which have taken place in the lives of many children just days after receiving their vaccinations.

I knew a mother who continued taking her child to receive his vaccinations despite the fact her intuition was screaming NO!!!! She now has a severely brain-damaged son. His body worked so hard to rid itself of the toxic ingredients of that shot, the fever ended up frying his brain. Now, at eight years of age, he endures countless grand-mal seizures on a daily basis, cannot speak, cannot control his bladder or bowels, and must be fed because he doesn't have the capacity to hold a spoon properly.

She's not the only mother who has cried out in despair at the damage done to her vaccinated child...

Richelle, after receiving shots at six months old went into shock-like behavior within ten hours of injection followed by a grand mal seizure with severe diarrhea and respiratory arrest. She is now severely mentally and physically handicapped.

Mark, after receiving shots at four months old began projectile vomiting, staring, and behavior changes within 12 hours of injection. He died within 26 hours.

Sean, after receiving shots at 8 months old began having reactions within 3 hours; swelling at the site of the injection, high-pitched screaming, projectile vomiting, diarrhea, and behavior change. He now has a learning disability with severe motor damage.

Christopher, after receiving shots at two months of age began

reacting within two hours, starting with high-pitched screaming. After short periods of sleep, interrupted by high-pitched
screaming, he died 21 hours from the moment he was injected.

Anna, after receiving shots at 15 months of age, was limping
within two days. Over the next two weeks she stopped walking,
developed unusual cold symptoms, a 102 degree fever, and was
irritable, wanting to be held constantly. Over the next six weeks,
she became totally paralyzed. At eight years of age, Anna cannot walk independently, remains paralyzed in her lower body,
and has processing delays.

Ashley, after receiving shots at 18 months old, began reacting
within 72 hours with a 103 degree fever and lethargy. She was
hospitalized with kidney failure and encephalitis. She is now
severely mentally and physically handicapped.

Kimberlie, after receiving shots at 2 months of age began
reacting within 3 hours with a 103 degree fever, high-pitched
screaming, and convulsions. She died of cardiac arrest shortly
thereafter.

Joshua, after receiving shots at 6 months old began reacting
within 6 hours with high-pitched screaming, did not want to be
held, a 101 degree fever followed by a one hour grand mal
seizure. Today he lives with moderate to severely mental retar-
dation and severe language delay.

We have been conditioned to vaccinate our children and, at
intervals, are informed by the public health department of yet
another "necessary" vaccine for our little ones. Like obedient
robots, most mothers show up just when their children turn the
age that the pimp persuaded the prostitute to dictate a mother's
participation.

Don't let the disguise of professionalism fool you. And don't
let their statistics persuade you into thinking your child is better
off being immunized, regardless the risks. When sad stories like
those above happen to you or your child, the risks are 100%.

When I get letters like the one below, I am scared for the children who depend soley on a mother who is not in her primal power....

"Do you think I need to know a lot about the vaccines and the dangers, etc? I know vaccines are bad in my heart, but what to say to someone who thinks they stop diseases is my concern. If vaccines seem to help stop death, doesn't that say something, or are they just dying of cancer instead? How sad, if this is so! But, would just as many have died of these diseases is the question. I need to take my baby back for her next shots in less than two months."

If our hearts say NO, that's good enough. Mother hearts don't lie. They only cringe when not listened to; and everyone suffers as a result. For books on the truth behind vaccinations, please call Nature's First Law at 1-800-205-2350.

While on the subject of women acting like robots, circumcision is still raking in the dough while raping our sons of their foreskin. And don't think that the only money to be made is in the procedure itself. The sale of foreskins for the purpose of skin graphs is a multi-million dollar business! How about that? The medical profession is so unprofessional they don't even give mothers a receipt for their son's foreskin! I'm not trying to be funny, but sometimes a sense of humor amidst a gross act of violence is the very thing which lures our anger to the surface, thereby empowering us with enough emotional energy and courage to protect our children in every way.

One day a woman called me to vent her anger. After much argument with her husband, she finally gave up in the defending of her newborn son. She sat in the waiting room and cried the whole time her son was in the other room, strapped down and screaming while some stranger took a knife to his penis. When I asked her why she allowed this nightmare to occur she immediately came to the defense of her husband saying, "What could I do? It's HIS child, too."

Perhaps someday her son will grow up to write a letter like this one that I recently received...

"When I studied circumcision I became aware of my deep scars and the ramifications of that act of genital mutilation. I no longer use knives on my food because knives are for circumcision. Knives are a reminder to me of my missing part. When I see a knife, I cringe."

And just yesterday I received a phone call from a sixty-five year old Jewish man from New York City who has recently awakened to his own anger at having been circumcised in the name of religion when he was first brought into this world.

I'm here to defend men in their right to be whole, and I don't want to hear any religious doctrine that blesses such a barbaric act. We must tackle ourselves where we least want to look — into our views about religion and how we are literally shackled to the past and to the rules which continue to be played out from one generation to the next. My dear Jewish friend Laura Kaplan Shanley, author of **Unassisted Childbirth**, has something important to say about this subject:

"I am so offended by circumcision that it is difficult for me to even write about it. On any given day thousands of men will meet in support groups to vent their anger over having been circumcised without a choice in the matter. Over one third of the active members of the anti-circumcision movement are Jewish. On any given day at least one hundred routine infant circumcisions will result in complications, irreversible surgical trauma, penile loss or even death. I have no problem with Jews circumcising their own as long as the 'circumcisee' is a consenting adult. A week old infant is not a consenting adult. Religious freedom is not about inflicting your beliefs on others, regardless of whether or not the other is your child. Children grow up to be adults, and many, many Jewish men are angry that they were circumcised in the name of religion. For those who say a Jewish circumcision is more humane because the child is held by loved ones and given wine to drink, Jody McLaughlin who is the editor/publisher of **Compleat Mother** magazine replies, 'Are you telling me that it is more humane to be hurt in the presence of those who supposedly love and care about you? Are you saying that it is more humane if a child's first sexual experience involving another human being is associated with blood, pain, and alcohol?'"

As shocking as it may be to our western minds, little girls in other societies are routinely forced into a different form of circumcision — female clitorectomies. While the western world is condoning male circumcision with the excuse of cleanliness, other cultures are cutting out the clitoris of each and every young girl, assuring death to the power of female sexual pleasure. I am eternally grateful to organizations such as The Intact Network who work to save infants and children from the pain, torture, and destruction of genital mutilation. We need to stop the horror of sexual mutilation wherever it occurs on our planet.

It seems only fitting we should next touch on the subject of sexuality. One aspect of the anger that is addressed in support groups comprised of circumcised men is sexual sensitivity. Their non-circumcised counterparts are enjoying a level of sexual pleasure unknown to victims of the knife.

The foreskin acts as both lubricant and masseuse during intercourse creating a highly stimulating sensation. As a mother, I can attest to this difference between circumcised and non-circumcised males because my three-year-old intact son absolutely loves pulling and stretching his foreskin, a gleeful pride in his eyes and a smile on his face. I don't see this self-nurturing behavior in the lives of toddler victims of circumcision.

Circumcision is a primal wound that changes the course of a life. This crime, together with denial of the breast and separate sleeping quarters, defines the initial sexual experience for a huge percentage of society's population. Pornography is that party called together; the walking wounded who, addicted to eagle-spread models in magazines, search out the womb where everything was once just fine; the walking wounded who, starved of the sweet warmth of a mother's breast, stare dreamily at the sight of cleavage; the walking wounded who, frustrated at their inability to know intimacy, have sex with strangers who will only do it for pay; the walking wounded who, angry and anxious for the hatred they feel, rape and kill women and children.

Never underestimate the deep scars of sexual dysfuction. Indeed, these wounds have changed the course of many lives. And it is the purpose of this book to begin licking those wounds that they may heal, lighting the way for a new direction and a humane new world.

When it comes to sex I've been around the block a few times. But what good is going around the block if it's not in the right vicinity? Years of promiscuity resting atop a childhood of molestation has made me a fine candidate for knowing all about being on the wrong side of town. It has taken years of therapy to remove these layers of dysfunction, and there, sitting at the core, is a small red-haired girl in the corner, knees pulled up close to her face, and tears staining the floor.

This may seem like a cold way to begin a discussion on the warm pleasures of sex, but those beautiful pleasures cannot be had for those of us caked deep in sexual trauma. We all know the statistics — one in three girls will be molested, and the statistic on boys is catching up. And for those who did not receive the continuous closeness they needed in their infancy, or who also endured the trauma of circumcision, sexual molestation is a stinging salt being rubbed into the primal wound. Trust cannot grow under such conditions, thus children grow up to become dis-trusting adults who make their way out into the world in search of love.

My own search for love led me through a myriad of experiences resulting in abandonment, abortions, prostitution, and rape. When in 1984 I made the decision to become free of drugs and alcohol, it was in those rooms of A.A. where I learned that I am worthy of receiving all that I need. Those recovered alcoholics nurtured me in such a way that slowly, very slowly, trust began to grow in this wounded heart of mine.

That was thirteen years ago. Codependency recovery entered my sphere soon thereafter, and I was truly on my way to a deeper self-understanding. Trial and error, good therapists, and the determination to know primal love led me finally to a life of healthy sexuality. Today I can talk about intimacy because I know what it is.

True intimacy allows us to be ourselves completely: the screaming infant who demands to be held, the nursing babe whose eyes melt dreamily into its mother's soul, the defiant toddler who angrily defends her/his perception of life. If we can't be ourselves on all other fronts, how can we suddenly awaken to teaching a lover what we want sexually?

Many women relate to me when I talk about how I used to close my eyes and send telepathic messages to my partner in the hopes he would catch my drift and respond accordingly. No such response ever occurred. In fact, results were always the opposite. Our love-making session was consummated with a free-floating anxiety which deepened the wedge already made by love-making sessions prior.

Maybe this explains the dynamics of adolescent rebellion. Perhaps we tire out after the first few years of reacting violently at the denial of our birthright to mother. Our unanswered cries go underground, bubbling up years later disguised as regular and consistent requests for negative attention. After all, any attention is better than no attention. When, after going to these additional lengths to receive the love we need and the gift is not forthcoming, rebellion becomes buried alongside babyhood insistence and resignation becomes the norm. Out of this is born the frigid woman and the frustrated man.

Sexual energy is our very life force. It's the beginning, the middle, and the everlasting connection to intimacy. Healthy sexuality swings wide the gates to Heaven — that river within which rushes from one powerful moment in time to the next.

When I finally learned to express my desires in such a way that the ears of my lover could hear, I was re-connected to an inner power I only vaguely remember from somewhere back in time. Healthy sexuality has brought me home to myself.

Probably the most challenging thing about coming home to our sexuality is getting in touch with exactly when we want to be sexual. Prior to motherhood, I tended to make myself available, regardless of my level of arousal. It made for great opportunities to please a man, but all the while I would be thinking about the food budget and such — my mind wasn't really on having sex. In the end, the only thing which grew out of these disconnected experiences in "intimacy" was resentment.

When I became pregnant there arose in me a feeling of protection, and sex was the furthest thing from my mind. My partner at the time was hardly supportive of this abstinence and I obligingly made myself sexually available on a few occasions until my prenatal instincts kicked in so strongly I refused to continue this compliant behavior.

I have talked to women who found pregnancy to be a time of high libido and active sexuality. Through all three of my pregnancies I craved sensuality — kissing, cuddling, massage — but not the vim and vigor of intercourse. It just didn't feel right to me. Even right up to the moment of Matthew's birth, when I was massaging myself to orgasm with each contraction, it was a totally separate experience from the penetrating act of intercourse. I share my experience and perception on this subject of sexuality in pregnancy not because I feel that my path is correct, but rather, because I know of too many other women like myself who have violated their maternal cue to sidestep sexuality once they have conceived. I want them to know they are not alone in their preference to abstain sexually.

And I know even more women who felt rushed into a return to sexual activity soon after the birth of their baby, before her own libido requested such behavior. Here she is, heavily in love with her newborn, nursing with every fiber of her being, giving

of herself in all ways to her completely helpless and totally lov-
able offspring. And she's being asked to divert her energy so as
to satisfy the sexual desires of her partner. I don't think so! This
is where the valuable role of a man steps in. Somebody needs to
nurture this women who is devoting herself TOTALLY to the
raising of humanity. Somebody needs to kiss her softly, massage her shoulders, hug her from the depths of his heart, be in
full gratitude for the unselfish role she plays in the human experience. Somebody needs to take unabashed pride in her. That
somebody should be the other somebody she sleeps with. That
somebody should not be a constant irritant who makes her all-
consuming life even more stressful. Somebody needs to grow
up by first recognizing his unwillingness to participate in this
most unselfish act of family nurturance stems from the unconscious jealousy that arises at the sight of the mother/infant bond.

Yes, jealousy. That little boy inside is waking up to the reality of his own life-long anxiety; this new child called his son or
daughter is getting what he didn't get, and now he feels kicked
out of the lap which has, up until now, served as a surrogate
mother. These men need to cry, deeply. They need to take a turn
at our breasts and breathe in the sweet fragrance of our motherhood while consuming liquid love. And they need to be grateful their own child will not endure an infancy of neglect.

With proper emotional and domestic support from her partner,
a new mother will eventually feel the natural return of her sexual attraction and oh, what a flow of blessings await the man
who lives up to his role as nurturer to the mother who nurtures
her young. He can be assured of a receptive and appreciative
sexual partner for the simple reason that he has honored the
mother/infant bond.

This poem, from my book **Love Letters** was written upon the
return of my sexual appetite, one year after the birth of my
son....

TWO MEN

Two men, one on either side...
The one who came from deep within me
  now searching out my breasts
The other searches his heart in
  moments of coming deep within me.

Two men, one on either side...

The one relies on me
  a springboard to his future
The other contemplates
  diving into eternity with me

Two men, one on either side...

The one drinks in my milk
The other replenishes me
  with his own sacred juice

Two men, one on either side...

The one knows me as mother
The other calls me lover.

Sessions in sex are my ticket to unlimited thought. I love to relax totally into the visualization of a better world while my partner first kisses me from head to toe and then centers in on nursing from my vagina. My powerful orgasms to follow make me physically and emotionally receptive to a tender and prolonged round of intercourse. We each come away from this experience feeling personally empowered and collectively in tune. To really strengthen both your sexual/spiritual power AND your relationship to the dedicated partner in your life, I suggest my book **Everyday Erotica For The Totally Devoted Couple** (available through Nature's First Law at 1-800-205-2350).

It only makes sense that the more physically fit we are, the more we can enjoy our sexuality. My sexual nature is greatly animated when I am feeling good about my body. When I like what I see about myself, it is easier for me to recognize the attraction my partner is feeling toward me. Fitness comes from the combination of diet and physical activity. While fruitarianism offers us a reprieve from unwanted weight-gain, physical activity guarantees the sculpting of our natural beauty.

Physical activity is cumulative. Every task we perform and every movement we make can have a beneficial effect on our overall health. Given the typically busy life of a mother, it is vital we incorporate physical activity so our personal needs are met in the context of daily life.

Throughout my first pregnancy I swam and jogged daily. When Sarah Lee was born I brought her in the pool and by one week of age she was resting on my upper back, clinging to my hair, while I swam laps. When I jogged, she slept blissfully in the baby sling. Becoming mother to three posed a new challenge for my exercise regime. I invested in both a jogging stroller and a child bike-cart. With baby Matthew in the backpack, toddler Jasmine in the jogging stroller, and big sister Sarah Lee sporting her pink roller-skates, I ran several miles each day. Since I elected not to own a car in the first year of being mother to three I relied heavily on my bike and child bike-cart. All three of my children fit comfortably in the front of the cart, and I had space enough in the back to accommodate books from the library, fruits from the produce market, or whatever else we needed to bring on home.

I love sharing my fitness program with my children. When we're not riding bikes or jogging together, then it's dancing and gymnastics. Every night we practice our handstands, stretch out, do yoga, and dance to our favorite tunes. As babies, all of my children have especially loved for me to dance while they were snugly tucked into their sling.

At night, when my children are asleep, I top off my day with a session of dancing, jogging on my bouncer, and a few yoga stretches. This nocturnal ritual in self-nurturing is my way of saying good-night to another beautiful day of loving myself, raising my children, and fulfilling my responsibility as a woman who cares deeply about the fate of humanity.

Chapter 8

HOMESCHOOLING
Befriending Our Blossoming Children

*"Doing all day what they love
lets them become their true selves."*
— **Richard Bach**, *Jonathan Livingston Seagull*

While watching another glorious Hawaiian sunset, with Matthew leaning over my shoulder from his snug place on my back and Jasmine enjoying each push of the swing, we all counted to one hundred — that's homeschooling. After we got home I read several stories to my three beautiful children — that's homeschooling. This morning greeted Sarah Lee with the responsibility of taking care of her horse — that's homeschooling. And they all pitched in with household chores — that's homeschooling.

I love to homeschool! It's so simple and so rewarding, as is natural hygiene, fruitarianism, breastfeeding, bonding, primal birthing, and self-governing pregnancy. Why not have the strawberries in your mothering smoothie be just as flavorful, just as vital, as the smoothie itself?

Given the fact that our brain is the survival organ for the human species, it isn't surprising our children are like thirsty sponges, soaking up everything going on around them...which is exactly why I find it so important to surround my children with only the best. And I happen to think the best is in the home of our very own family where they are embraced throughout the day by the people who love them the most.

The first question people ask me when they find out that my children are homeschooled is, "But that's not legal, is it?" This question hits me at two levels — emotional and rational.

These kindred spirits made a soulful choice to be under my wing. In the same way that their bodies do not belong to the food and drug administration, nor the medical establishment, their minds don't belong to the state and nearest public or private school. My response to this question of legality resembles the answer given by the Messiah in Richard Bach's profound book **Illusions**. When a radio announcer asked if there isn't something illegal about flying around the country in an ancient airplane, taking people for rides, the Messiah simply stated: "No one can stop us from what we want to do."

And so it is with managing the education needs of our young. No one can stop us from giving them the space to become their true selves.

Though each state has its own hoops of policies and procedures, homeschooling IS legal. In fact, the popularity of homeschooling is growing rapidly as parents become increasingly concerned about the quality of their children's daily lives. Juvenile delinquency, gangs, alcohol and other drugs, sexual pressure, teen pregnancy, weapons, slashings, murder, and suicide now coincide with school's daily curriculum. Surprising but true, more than 200,000 children carry guns to school each day, and over 2,000 children are physically attacked on school grounds every hour!

History is stacked with many great minds who were nurtured in the privacy of their own homes, by parents who themselves were without a formal education. Just to name a few who have reached their full potential as a result of bypassing the public education experience...John Quincy Adams, Pearl S. Buck, Winston Churchill, Sandra Day O'Connor, Isadora Duncan, Albert Einstein, Patrick Henry, Margaret Mead, General George

Patton, Astronaut Sally Ride, Theodore Roosevelt, Leo Tolstoy, George Washington, Daniel Webster, Alexander Graham Bell, Agatha Christie, Noel Coward, Thomas Edison, Benjamin Franklin, Douglas MacArthur, Wolfgang Mozart, William Penn, Franklin Roosevelt, George Bernard Shaw, Mark Twain, Martha Washington, and John Wesley.

Today, virtually all colleges — even the most selective of colleges — are known to accept homeschooled children who have never set foot in a classroom. In fact, young adults who were homeschooled consistently score higher on all college entrance exams than their public education counterparts.

There are as many approaches to homeschooling as there are families practicing this alternative path of education. Many organized religions have entire homeschooling programs which include textbooks and regular testing for determining progress, as well as private education institutes which offer home study courses. Because these alternatives to public education tend to emulate more the scheduling of compulsory curriculum than the freedom to learn, I don't feel that they create the necessary mood for true self-discovery.

I am of the "free-lance educator" variety. My children and I work together to create avenues for learning that are mutually satisfying. We use our local public library on a regular basis and always find answers to our most recent burning questions. We have so much fun as a homeschooling family that neighbors have gone so far as to call Child Protective Services because, according to these skeptics, my children couldn't possibly be getting a proper education, what with all the free time they have on their hands. Society and its "experts" have harassed us to no end. Their vehement attempts at intefering with my children's right to the natural unfolding of their talents has been an irritant to say the least.

Isadora Duncan, the founder of Modern Dance, was once quoted as saying, "It seems to me that the general education a child receives at school is absolutely useless." Isadora began teaching dance to neighbor kids by the tender age of six and by age ten, after convincing her mother that school was a complete waste of time, fully embraced her role as a dancer and a revolutionist. She owed it to the heroic and adventurous spirit of her mother that her vision of dance was not stifled, as it surely would have been in the time constraints and conservative personality of general education.

Free time is the single most important aspect to homeschooling! I teach my children to value their time to the extent that they are responsible for what goes into a given hour, day, week, month, year, and lifetime. Homeschooling allows a family to clarify their values, then live up to those values, unimpeded by the ignorance which drives the public sector. It must be quite confusing, for instance, for a vegetarian child to be given ethical and health reasons not to eat meat while the teachers and school textbooks discuss animal products as a necessary part of nutrition.

My favorite component of homeschooling lies in the act of family involvement. Responsibility to one another and the daily contribution to growth and maintenance of our family system imparts great opportunities for my children to feel important and valuable. The family-oriented societies in our world today, untainted by the formal schooling mentality, enjoy a much higher level of sibling symbiosis by virtue of the fact that older children are given much responsibility toward their younger sisters and brothers. There is not the age discrimination often found as early as age five and even younger, where schools organize pupils according to age, and a cultist attitude culminates as a result of reduced exposure to and tolerance for children of other, especially younger, ages. According to anthropologist Margaret Mead, "One of the most serious deprivations in our culture is that children so rarely have the opportunity to care for smaller children. Thus they do not learn the ingredients of nurturing to prepare them to be parents when their time comes."

Family responsibility includes management of home, health,

and finances. Helping with household chores is a wonderful way to bring about feelings of belonging and value into the lives of our children. Helping them to embrace and appreciate the gentle, nurturing qualities of fruitarianism ensures their undefiled childhood and a superbly healthful future. Helping our children understand regular and consistent financial outlays will contribute to their eye for realism so that they may recognize consumerism from a standpoint of efficiency, sequencing, and the power of choice, and not be left to "want it all" with no way of knowing how to make that happen. We can teach our children to use their intuition along with their intellect when making consumerist decisions.

Once again, as was plainly seen in the chapter on bonding, the challenge of togetherness arises. Homeschooling is a lifestyle of daily contact. Home businesses are great because our children can partake of the responsibilities and rewards of our family's financial independence. I think it's wonderful for our children to observe the dynamics of earning a living. Perhaps one of the reasons why my generation has limped along financially, by resorting so easily to public assistance, is because we didn't have the "family farm" or "Mom and Pop store" background our parents and grandparents so often recollected from their own childhoods. Instead, we only HEARD our parents discuss their need to work. We didn't actually observe the act of work.

In a society where private business is available for reaping the rewards of financial independence, it's fun to watch our children get the hang of earning a living. Entrepreneurship is a learned behavior requiring motivation and discipline. Promoting our service or product, replenishing our supplies, and managing our profits are lessons which can begin with something so simple as a lemonade stand.

Through us, our children can learn the many ways to make ends meet. For instance, the beauty of bartering. Public school economics classes seldom teach our children how to trade anything but money. While at a second-hand store Sarah Lee, who was eight years old at the time, fell in love with a bike which cost $75.00. I didn't have enough money and told her that if she really wanted the bike, I trusted she would figure a way to generate her own determination. I left her in deep thought and went about my business of shopping. Several minutes later I saw her talking with the store manager. They motioned me over.

It turned out that my determined daughter struck up a deal whereby she could take the bike home now, and contribute her time helping at the store to the tune of $4.00 an hour until the bike was paid off. Sarah Lee triumphantly wheeled that lavender bicycle with the unicorn banana-seat out the front door as I walked behind her in awe and respect.

Sarah Lee was just a few months old when I first read about homeschooling. The idea of keeping my child at home made so much sense to the primal mother in me I didn't question it for a moment. Still, I was scared.

How could I possibly be able to teach my children what teachers spend four years in college learning to teach? My degree in Sociology hardly rendered me eligible for teaching the likes of reading, writing, and arithmetic! My funny-bone was struck while asking that question as it suddenly occurred to me that, before a child reaches kindergarten their parents have successfully taught them to speak and comprehend one or more languages, to count, to use silverware, to dress, to use the potty, to swim, to ride a bike, to roller-skate, to share with friends, to enjoy story-time, even how to tie their shoe laces.

This poem by Laura Kaplan Shanley gives us an inside view of the potential mastery which lives within the minds of our children, and the simple, benign role we play in helping them to establish self-determination.

ALMOST
I know how to tie my shoe
Cross the laces, pull one through
Make a little loop and then.....
Could you show me once again?

I know how to ride a bike —
But you could help me if you like
Hold me as I start out slow
Faster...faster...don't let go!

I DID IT!
I know how to tie my shoe
Cross the laces, pull one through
Make a little loop and then
Wrap it round and through again.

I know how to ride a bike —
But you could help me if you like
Hold me as I start out slow
Faster...faster...here I go!

I was fast becoming convinced that, with little effort, I could include the 3 R's into my parenting repertoire. I had no idea just how little effort it would take! By reading to my daughter everyday — pointing to each word as I read — she soon developed a sense of association and, to my complete surprise, while riding at the back of the town bus at the curious age of six, Sarah Lee proudly and loudly sounded out each and every profane word inscribed across the metal backing of the seat directly in front of us. As she gleefully asked if she got the words right I vacillated between parental pride and public embarrassment. Everyone on the bus turned to glare at the cussing child sitting next to me. They had no idea what an honor this was, to be inadvertently invited to my little girl's first reading recital!

The most popular criticism against homeschooling has to do with the issue of socialization. It is believed that socialization skills can only develop in a school setting. My children have been socializing with me since their days of preconception, and socializing with each other from birth on. Where do people get this notion that the steady dose of a large group of people makes for a better social human? On the contrary, intimacy is the foundation of loving socialization and the close, consistent, and nurturing contact between family members. Making love successfully does not require an orgy background, and socialization development is not defined by crowded classrooms and concrete courtyards.

The natural unfolding of our children is often violated by the academic assumptions and expectations of our culture. In Joseph Chilton Pearce's book **The Magical Child** he delivers to us a far more humane approach to meeting the educational needs of our young, simply by recognizing the natural unfolding of the human brain and the necessary pre-requisite known as play.

Play, which is the child's greatest intelligence, cannot develop unless they are played with. Telling them stories, singing songs to them, twirling them about, chasing waves together along the ocean's shore, and giving children of all ages the freedom to play together all day long, not just when some authority figure sounds a bell and dismisses them to fifteen minutes in a concrete setting...these are the ingredients of play.

The play of baby animals has to do with the conditions the animal will meet in its adult life. As humans, we begin our climbing career at an early age in preparation for the foraging creature that we are. When given the opportunity, little boys will easily practice the nurturing behavior associated with doll-play, but instead they are usually given "action figures" whose sole responsibility it is to decimate the enemy. Toy manufacturers create an environment which perverts Nature's Plan as regards the trait of aggression. Natural aggression and defense instincts help humans to be complete in their self-authority, and these instincts are equally powerful in both genders. Their respective natures may differ, but they exist and are true. The human animal is a frugivore without natural predators, yet life in its daily context sometimes consists of adversity. Though our peaceful nature is the result of our excellence, we also have the biological inclination to defend ourselves if necessary; a biological inclination, however, which does not require that we inundate our sons with toy weaponry. When children awake in the morning, the first thing they want to do is pick up where they left off the night before and play, play, play. Getting ready for a school-bus denies them this biological decree. Instead, along with the overwhelming majority of children in society, they resignedly rise from their warm beds and feed their brains with a few early-morning violence-oriented cartoons accompanied by a huge bowl of sugary cereal, before heading out to catch a ride away from a day otherwise designed by Nature to be mostly about play.

Speaking of television....television is another form of imprisonment whereby the playful child is held at bay from herself. According to Joseph Chilton Pearce, "With television, the damage comes not from the content, but medium. We shouldn't have television for the early child. It floods the child's brain with a prepared audio-visual image at the time when the brain's great job is to create imagery from within."

Three times in my mothering career, for a grand total of three months, I have brought a television into our home. Each time the results were EXACTLY the same. Precious minutes and hours of creative play and human interaction were lost to the hypnotic state of television viewing.

Mothers are always remarking at how lucky I am to not have a television. Luck has nothing to do with it. Courage and persistence is what has kept television out of the lives of my children. Given the fact most of these mothers say their husbands would never allow for a television-free environment, I can only remind the primal mother in us that we are responsible for doing what is best for our children and not for acquiescing on behalf of our partners.

As women, we have been raised not to question the desires of men — only to honor them. But the desires of these last few generations are born out of childhood deprivation which has led to a hunger instead of wholeness. We cannot help our children, ourselves, or our partners if we are tied into going against our heart in favor of avoiding the conflict which generally follows when we disagree with the insistence of our partners and instead defend the true needs of our children. In truth, our children are our partners. They came through us with the expectation to have their needs met. There can be no stronger partnership than what takes place between a mother and her child.

I was once asked to guest lecture on the subject of feminism at a university in Oklahoma. This was at the time of the Persian Gulf war. In my talk, I focused on the role of a mother to create a healthy and safe environment for her family. The example I used was an ongoing event which was taking place in my own home. This was one of the three television-owning episodes I had encountered in my mothering career. My then-boyfriend's attention was completely glued to the screen, watching every-thing which had to do with the ongoing war. There, inside the four walls of home where I dedicated my life to raising a peace-loving human being, were the sounds of gun-shots, blood-cur-dling screams, murder, and commentary.

Something was wrong with this picture! When I approached the subject, he vehemently professed his right to keep up with the news, despite the fact that this constant onslaught of warring was having an adverse affect on both myself and my daughter. Enough she-bearing on my part, and he finally plugged in the earphones, turned the television screen away from the center of attention, and proceeded to further feed his soul with violence. At least we were no longer being forced to partake of the same meal.

After sharing this story with the audience, a few men raised their fists at me and defended the man in my life for having a right to watch anything he chooses. Not once did these irate students reflect on the frightening affects this television viewing was having on my child. I reminded these men of the imperative role that women play in the lives of their children, to which their only response was "Fuck you!"

When I finished speaking and everyone was leaving, several women students milled around, pretending like they were putting things away — ever so slowly. When finally the last male had left the room these women began to cry and asked me how they could regain control over the lives of their own children, their hearts were aching to be listened to yet their entire lives were managed by the desires of their men. They too wanted to shield their young from this barrage of media violence.

Violence is a serious problem in the lives of our men. Little boys grow up awry, and it all begins at the beginning. The United States has the largest prison population of any nation in the world; a population that is mostly male. Domestic violence is an epidemic; most of the aggressors are male. The extent of child sexual molestation is beyond our wildest imaginations; most of the perpetrators are male. Rape is real and happens every day; most of the rapists are male. When we don't give our little boys what they need, dirty waters become their only quench for thirst. And we all suffer.

Men need to heal, and women need to help them...but not in the way we have attempted to up until now; walking on eggshells, maintaining the status quo, being afraid to disagree, being even more afraid to take a stand. Our little boys need the comfort and security of a primal mother, a female who will fight tooth and nail to maintain a loving bond with her little son. Homeschooling is an important way to keep them safe from a society where aggressive behavior is the norm. When they grow up and walk out into that wayward world, they will be peacemakers with a purpose rather than trouble-makers who haven't a clue as to the source of their frustration.

Healthy self discipline is the by-product of enjoying one's discipline in life. What does that mean? According to Webster's Dictionary, discipline is defined as "a regimen that develops or improves a skill." To ponder over the fact most of the people who have made the grandest contributions to humanity did not have a formal education is to confirm the fact that freedom inside childhood leads to self-discovery in its highest form. When our children are given the space and time to be all they desire to be, little outside discipline is required because our children are excitedly disciplined in what they love.

When Sarah Lee first began gymnastics, she practiced no less than five hours daily in our livingroom. When she decided to create a horse-lover's newsletter I had to make reservations to get on my word processor! Just like our growing babies don't need to be disciplined into walking and our free-spirited toddlers don't need to be disciplined into living up to the degree of play necessary for optimum development, our older children don't need to be disciplined about what matters most to them. When children are full-throttle in their own sprouting talents they are not producing attention-getting behavior. On the contrary, they get our FULL attention as we enjoy feelings of total respect and awe for their magnificent abilities!

For most mothers, discipline is a tricky subject. Having come from generations past who believed in physical punishment, we find ourselves trying to sit on hands that are culturally ingrained to swat, or holding back words that would most certainly wound our little ones. I make my share of mistakes, I do the best I can, and I always strive to do better. Some days go great, other days feel like a total loss. I keep in mind what Alfie Kohn, author of **Punished By Rewards** says: "There is a difference between forgiving ourselves as occasional blunders and refusing to admit that certain approaches ARE blunders."

We usually repeat the kind of discipline we were brought up

with. It is important to sort out the past and heal from whatever abuse occurred while in the care of parents who were simply repeating what they had experienced in their own childhoods. In Vimala McClure's beautiful book **The Tao Of Motherhood** she eloquently writes, "Healthy parenting is especially challenging when our own childhoods weren't healthy. It requires energy, attention, and constant restraint. Realize that you need healing. Take time out to nurture yourself."

I take my self-nurturing needs VERY seriously. I rely on soothing baths or long, warm showers as a way to nurture myself when the going gets rough. Those few minutes to myself, nurtured by the healing properties of warm water — otherwise known as recreating life in the womb — completely transforms my attitude and I come out feeling energized and ready for another round of raising my young.

Another way I nurture myself is by making sure I spend time every day doing what I love...writing and dancing. At night, after we have read inspirational books in the comfort of our family bed and my children have all fallen asleep, I slip away to the kitchen where I spend the next three hours dancing with ear-phones on while writing at my word processor. I must feed my own spirit if I want to be a role model of a happy woman for my children. When I strive to become better in my own world, everything and everyone around me becomes better too. Gloria Steinem reminds us, "Having healthy core self-esteem is like having strong roots. We can bend with the wind and still sur-vive." Nurturing ourselves by doing what we love is fertile ground for building healthy core self-esteem.

Because the books we read to our children have a profound effect on their perception of life, it is important we choose their soul-food with as much integrity as we choose the foods which meet their body's nutritional needs. Our family loves allegories such as **Jonathan Livingston Seagull** by Richard Bach, **The Alchemist** by Paulo Coelho, and **Hind's Feet In High Places** by Hannah Hurnard.

The best disciplinary measures are those which come out of our searching for the true meaning behind the behavior of our children. In many cases their actions and attitudes mirror what is taking place in our own psyches. Jasmine, now five years old, mysteriously acts out all the nuances of my inner child healing. You can well imagine how irritating this can be for me! Before we can enjoy the maturity of responding lovingly to our children's behavior we must first become willing to delve into the realness of their own experience so we can understand exactly how they feel, then go on that archaeological dig whereby we heal the child within our own psyches who was reacted to by a parent in much the same way that we are at the moment feeling led to react. When we delve into the realness of our own childrens' experience, and see the angelic innocence and primal curiosity which most often accompanied our own childhood actions, we can then accept the fact we never deserved the harsh discipline we received as children. With this new perception of an old experience, this paradigm shift, we can then delve into the realness of our own childrens' experience and have a deeper understanding of their reasons for doing what they do. A sense of profound freedom comes from this deeper understanding, and our children greatly appreciate being both understood and honored for who they are.

Freedom is a beautiful thing. Early each morning my children and I lie in our big family bed and watch the changing colors of a Hawaiian sky. In the faint distance we hear the crossing guard's whistle and children scurrying from the warmth of home to the scheduling of school. I greet these mornings with a deep sense of gratitude for my courage to homeschool.

Some mornings one or more of my children are still asleep when society's school bell rings. Forrest Carter, in his wonderful book **The Education Of Little Tree** writes, "A man rises of his own will in the morning." Like natural hygiene teaches our children to trust when they are hungry, homeschooling offers our children the sleep patterns that are fine-tuned to their psychological and physiological needs. By creating an environment of natural unfolding we are actually fostering in our children a vision of their own Greatness. We must help our children develop ALL of their skills, psychic skills included.

When Sarah Lee was still a crawling baby she performed an act in psychic phenomenon at our local book-store that to this day leaves me awe-struck. At a corner booth I noticed a woman crying. With Sarah Lee in the baby sling, I went over to console the woman as she began telling me she just learned her mother was dying of cancer. In that instant, Sarah Lee crawled out of the sling, down to the floor, and away from the booth where we were sitting. I didn't think much of it because we frequented this place and Sarah Lee always made herself right at home. A few minutes later, when she had yet to return from the book aisles, I went in search of her.

There she was, coming out from the back of the store, clutching a paperback book in her hand as she crawled clumsily in my direction.

As I bent over to pick her up she went right on past me until reaching the woman's booth. Once there, she pulled herself to her feet and handed the book to this grieving woman. The title? **How To Survive The Loss Of A Parent**.

Visualization skills is another extremely important tool for our growing children. For her ninth birthday, Sarah Lee wanted a Persian cat. I showed doubt as she proceeded to commit to the manifestation of something we could not afford. When I saw her combing through the "Free Cats" section of our local newspaper I gently mentioned that people don't tend to give away Persian cats. That didn't dissuade her. A few days later (have you ever noticed a manifestation generally occurs a few days later, once we become completely committed to making it happen?), while talking with a local merchant, I mentioned we were looking for an adult neutered cat for Sarah Lee's birthday. The store owner happily remarked, "Well, actually, I have a wonderful cat that hasn't been getting enough attention since I got my new dog. I would be honored if Sarah Lee became her new owner!" When I asked if her cat had long hair she proudly replied, "Of course, he's a Persian." I could see the look of victory in Sarah Lee's eyes as we made arrangements to have "Barong" brought to our home the next morning.

In perhaps the most mind-stretching book I have ever read, **The Celestine Prophecy** by James Redfield, he writes "Accepting the idea that reality is an outgrowth of mental intention gives us back our power, and promises hope for the future." The only way our children can truly believe in their ideas and hopes is if we allow them to follow their own hearts, to listen to that different drummer beating steadily inside them. We are responsible for making a difference in our own lives so as to be excellent role models in the lives of our children. They, in turn, will have the advantage of seeing themselves in a most brilliant light. If we simply reconcile ourselves to society as it stands today and spend all our time getting our children to accommodate themselves to it, then nothing will change and our children will have no choice but to do the same with their children.

As children, before conformity caught a hold of us, we knew who we were and what we loved. My book **Anatomy Of An Accomplishment** is devoted to this truth. By the age of four I was clearly aware that my purpose involved speaking, writing, and dancing on behalf of revealing the great potential of humanity.

Self-determination is the greatest gift we can impart to our children; teaching them to believe in themselves, promising them the moon, and then showing them the way to reach their dreams.

John Lennon's mother was once known to tell him, "Well, John, playing guitar is well and fine, but you can't make a living at it." We are fortunate that he did not take her opinion to heart; otherwise, we wouldn't have his beautiful song "Imagine" to remind us of the joy which awaits a peaceful world.

Of all the mothering decisions our heart asks of us, home-schooling is one of the most challenging; partly because of its place in the sequence of events. When a woman has fought upstream against the likes of professionals, partners, and personal fears through the seasons of self-governing pregnancy, sovereign birth, mother/infant bonding, child-led breastfeeding...when she has said NO to cooked foods, vaccinations, and circumcision...when she has embraced raw plant foods and fruitarianism, and trusted the principles of natural hygiene — depending on the degree of personal empowerment she has developed along the way — she may feel overwhelmed at the idea of going to battle one more time, where the battlefield is bigger than ever. I close this chapter with a letter depicting the ongoing struggle of my aspiring primal mothering sisters...

"I have been struggling with the homeschooling issue for some time. I'm still not sure what we're going to do. My heart's telling me one thing and I hear myself saying and doing things that I don't believe. Me and my husband have struggled with so many parenting issues already."

Freelance learning is to the developing mind what breastfeeding is to the growing baby — natural, nice, and biologically decreed. To understand this biological reality is to recognize the reasons why curriculum-based education away from the loving security of their home is a double whammy to the psyches of our young.

I always entrust my heart to make final decisions affecting my children, regardless the conflict it creates in my other relationships, biological fathers included. If nature went so far as to hold us women responsible for building, birthing, breastfeeding, and bonding to our babies, surely we are also equipped with every other necessity required for their welfare.

The computer bank for all this valuable information is in our hearts. Listen to your heart...it's telling you what you need to hear.

Chapter 9

MOTHER AND CHILD REUNION
Our Only Ticket Home

"The only thing that shatters dreams is compromise."
— **Richard Bach**

Seventy percent of all American children under age four are in daycare. One million children a year now are hospitalized for brutal beatings by their parents or caretakers. Five thousand are killed outright by their parents between the ages of two weeks and two years. One out of three children under the age of sixteen are sexually molested. The United States has the highest teenage suicide rate in the world.

And the primal mother is accused of being over-protective! We must ALWAYS be in a protective mode with our children. Paranoia is a primal thing, and it's the ONLY thing we have to go on — unless, of course, we want to wait until there is enough evidence to prove our children are hurting behind our backs. By then, the damage has been done, the trust level in our child has diminished, and we are left with feelings of remorse.

It's not easy for women to rear up and growl back at a patriarchal empire that is temporarily in control. I say "temporarily" because the only hope for humanity is the restoration of collective feminine wisdom and strength. When the men (partners, preachers, physicians, principals, etc.) in our lives challenge our mothering instincts, it becomes our task to muster up the courage necessary to defend the innate rights of our offspring.

Many women are struggling just to stay alive inside domestic violence, and have no energy left to defend their children against the same. Every year thousands of women die at the hands of their lovers. Domestic violence is a progressive disease. Women who are caught in this trap live between the extremes of running away with their children and returning to the scene of the crime. Statistics show that these women leave an average of eleven times before finally getting out, dead or alive. Their children witness this horrendous behavior and assimilate it as the norm. Little chance do they have of creating a life different than what they have endured. Girls grow up to be subservient, and that stance of subservience brings out the bully in the men they attract. And the vicious cycle carries itself into yet another generation.

As primal mothers, we have the grand opportunity to be a role model of strength for our children, not a role model of submission. The only authority in our mothering career lives inside the messages dictated by our heart. Question all others who claim authority, and stop questioning the true authority which makes no claims. It knows. Just like an elephant doesn't need to question its massive strength, neither do we need to question the value of information emanating from our hearts.

Primal mothering is non-negotiable. It just is. When we hear ourselves say, "I'd love to, but my husband..." we need to stop long enough to remember exactly who we are in the life of our children. We are the she-bear with biologically directed orders. We are the driver of this vehicle called the human experience. We are the solution to this sad world. And right now we need to plunge in and protect our children from drowning in a sea of social neglect.

If your religion tells you that the man is the head of the household, then you better start questioning your religion. Males have their part to play in it, but decision-making needs to be up to women. Other female animals don't accept interference from their male counterparts when it comes to their mothering decisions. Our children deserve no less than what nature planned for them — a primal mother who listens to the dictates of her heart.

If your employer tells you that you can't return to work with your newborn, challenge such rhetoric. Women have brought humanity through thousands upon thousands of years with children in tow. No job is impossible to the woman who commits to primal mothering.

Joseph Chilton Pearce pleads, "Women need to take their newborns into the workplace. We need women's base intelligence in every walk of life."

We may need to shake up our external world in order to maintain vigilence to our inner call. I have been called a martyr, and I can see now that I am. According to Webster's Dictionary, a martyr is a person who willingly suffers death rather than renounces her or his religion. My religion is primal mothering and, yes, I would suffer death rather than renounce the rights of my children.

Truth is an extremist, and clarity regarding that truth creates power. It is true that an emphasis on the male has imbalanced our society and, if we want to change the course of humanity, our point of power is NOW.

Chapter 10

I AM WOMAN
Hear Me Roar

*"Females have just as much intellect as males,
but their tendency is toward predominance
of the intelligence of the heart, which works for the
well-being and continuity of the species. It's a deep
and kind of an unknown, almost mysterious thing,
which worries males."* — **Joseph Chilton Pearce**

We can comb through the history books in search of the roots
to female oppression, but precious time would slip by. And this
world cannot afford to lose any more time. The bigger picture
will present itself as we go along. For now, our job is to take a
look at where we are and do something about getting to where
we need to be.

We must stop perpetuating submissive females and oppres-
sive males. Instead of whining about the plight of this planet,
we need to engage our feminine power and enact change, beginning with our own family systems. To whine is to side with
powerlessness, to roar is to live from our primal core.

We can't save the world until we have first saved the very sol-
diers needed to save the world — women. To bring the feminine
touch back to humanity is to bring humanity back to itself. It
takes a lot of courage to heal from submissiveness. It takes
developing a belief in ourselves after generations of genetic

encoding that we are the inferior gender, incapable of making valuable decisions. Keep in mind, it wasn't that many years ago when women were not allowed to vote!

How interesting that the word "coddle" means to cook in water just below the boiling point. When we coddle the men in our lives, when we silently go along with things that our heart is dead-against, we are creating relationships that live just below the boiling point. Simmering turns to resentment and the next thing we know, we are angry over the littlest things. Many failed relationships have women admitting that they finally reached their boiling point and men saying, "I don't know what happened!"

What happened is we didn't stand up for how we really felt. We allowed ourselves to be lost in the confusion of agreeing for the sake of avoiding confrontation. How can we step out of this submissive behavior? One step at a time, remembering that the first step is always the hardest to take; it's the leap of faith. Faith that we can make our lives better by virtue of listening to our hearts.

The first step is to ascertain a level of safety in our home. If self-assertion will be met with physical violence, then we may need to vote with our feet and walk away. I walked away on the night of my four-year wedding anniversary. My then husband decided to turn his nose up at my special vegetarian dinner, leave his baby girl crying after him, and drive off with his drinking buddies for a game of basketball and a night of partying. After nursing Sarah Lee to sleep, I sat looking out at the late-night sky, knowing this anniversary would end in the violence which always accompanied his drinking bouts. I meditated deeply on my situation, then came to the conclusion that I had no intention of enduring another miserable wedding anniversary. At midnight, I packed my most valuable possessions, wrapped sleeping Sarah Lee in a blanket and placed her in the car-seat, then drove away from my marriage. My life could not truly begin until the nightmare had ended. My leap of faith that life could be better if I only was willing to take the plunge taught me a woman and her children are better off in a car contemplating their next step than in a home where fear runs the show.

Bringing our womanhood to the surface requires a dedication to the cause. The world cannot heal without our complete womanhood. And our children cannot be fully protected without the activated primal mother who lives inside our complete womanhood. When we make this dedication to the cause of becoming complete in our womanhood, we are sometimes required to make decisions contrary to emotional or financial convenience. Divorce is a reality that many women face. I never thought it would be a part of my reality, but then, I never realized the depth of responsibility which comes with raising children whose primal needs are being met at every turn. I had no idea all this mothering energy had previously been used to please a man. Now the time had come for this man to be exactly that...a man, and not another child who competed for my maternal energy.

How do we begin this process of transferring our energies back onto our children? By first becoming presumptuous. Let's presume we are right about what our mothering hearts are telling us. Let's presume men have the strength to survive being challenged. Let's presume only good can come from practicing primal mothering and living up to our total womanhood.

Next, let's get arrogant. According to Webster's Dictionary, arrogance is self-importance. Let's develop so much self-importance we can finally see how important we are to the salvation of humanity.

Every two seconds a child dies of starvation; that's 40,000 daily for a total of 60,000,000 this year alone. Guess how many people could be adequately fed by the grain saved if Americans reduced their intake of meat by just ten percent? Yes, if we cut our car trips to McDonalds and grocery-cart strolls down the meat aisle by just one-tenth, we would contribute to the saving of 60,000,000 children this year. With this in mind, imagine the huge impact total vegetarianism would have on deserving children around the world!

Total womanhood is about looking at this statistic and getting fired up to make change. If your child was dying in your arms tonight because there wasn't enough food in your body to produce milk, and there was nothing to give them in place of your dried-up breast, what do you think would be your highest priority in that moment? Sending a rocket to the moon? Balancing the federal budget? Testing a new bomb?

Tonight, thousands upon thousands of our sisters are going to look into the dying eyes of their starving children. It doesn't matter why. It only matters that it is happening. It's time to change the channel on male-dominated political games and start solving serious problems. It's time to start saving women and children.

We need to continually express the compassionate, human side of ourselves. We must develop the power to stop being small and selfish and make a difference in the world around us. By small I mean we must stop acting small in the face of such a large problem which humanity faces; by selfish I mean we must think beyond the comfort zone of not rocking the boat inside our own homes.

Global change begins at home. When we stand up for the rights of our own children we are throwing a pebble into a mighty sea where latent womanhood sleeps lightly, ready to wake up when enough sisters have said, "I care."

Dare to care. Our point of power is NOW!

Chapter 11

SEVENTH GENERATION MOTHERING
Harvesting A New Humanity

"When I look into the future, it's so bright it burns my eyes."
— **Oprah Winfrey**

An attitude of doom and gloom does not light the fire in our hearts. Yes, we've strayed considerably from our human roots. No, we have not strayed too far. Were that the case, dedicated primal mothers — warriors for this wayward world — would not be bubbling up through the layers of social dysfunction.

To have a vision for humanity is to have an undying faith in our ability to correct, knowing that our corrections will be pebbles rippling out and reaching far into the future.

Sports teams are such a fine example of last minute corrections and the powerful consequences that can follow. Many important games have been won by teams who were behind just minutes before the whistle blew. Having chosen an attitude of faith and fortitude, these team members re-grouped and came back stronger than ever. As primal mothers, that's what we need to do.

Ask yourself this question: If you had just five minutes to whisper into the consciousness of humanity the most important "play" for winning re-entry to Paradise, what words of wisdom would stream from your heart? I love this question. It draws out a strength and compassion in me that is magnanimous. The entirety of this book represents my answer to humanity's homecoming. But if I were in the huddle and had only five minutes to encourage my team, this is the play I am calling out:

Begin at once to simplify your life in such a way that mother/child togetherness is the cornerstone. Remove yourself from all submissive behavior, including that which involves your spouse, the medical industry, the food and drug administration, and organized religion. Wrap your arms around your blossoming belly, your newborn, your toddlers, your young children, your growing adolescents, and remind them daily that nothing compares to the joy of raising them into their own sovereignty. At night, while they sleep in this bosom of security, wrap your arms around yourself — dear woman — and breathe in the fragrance of your own sacredness. Know who you are and live that truth with every fiber of your being.

Now, what if we had five hundred years to coach humanity into following our cue? What if we acted as if we were here forever, watching our efforts bring forth the glow of transformation: a world without war, womanhood without oppression, childhoods without abandonment, manhood without violence, animals without fear of death, spirituality without religious chains, life without death...life without death?

Physical immortality is just as much our birthright as breastfeeding, continuous contact, fruitarianism, and superb health. Physical immortality requires a passion to continuously change and evolve, an excitement about living, a desire for real intimacy with other people, and a cellular connection with others on the planet who have made a similar commitment.

I love this excerpt from Joe Alexander's new book **A New Age Perspective On Art** when he discusses physical immortality....

"People say, of course, that death is natural and good. Everything dies eventually, even the bristlecone pine. If people didn't die, the world would get so crowded there'd be no place you could spit without getting somebody very mad at you. Well, you know how it is — no matter how much we say things to convince ourselves that death is natural and good, nobody really wants to die. If we were really convinced that there was some way to avoid death, we'd go for it. Now, mostly people are so stagnant and set in their skeptical ways that they'll never admit of the possibility that there might actually be some way not to die. Anyone who would even entertain the idea is a loony bird, in the minds of the vast majority. However — I have experienced enough ascension, enough revitalization and rejuvenation, that I am willing to entertain the possibility. I have experienced the fact that it is possible to become more fully alive, so, maybe one could become eternally alive."

"I think most people have never experienced any sustained and consistent ascension, they have never worked seriously at becoming more abundantly alive in terms of spiritual energy; everyone does seek more abundance in terms of money and property of course. But all most people have ever known, in the spiritual sense, is stagnation and gradual decline, so the idea of ascension, rejuvenation, and immortality is very strange, like a fantasy."

"Even so, physical immortality is, paradoxically, the only real solution to overpopulation. See, if you start practicing ascension, with the hope of achieving immortality, you'll become much more intelligent and responsible, and you'll start to have enough sense to see what the causes of all our problems are and how to really solve them, overpopulation being one of them. Only people working on ascension will ever have enough sense to figure out how to solve the problem of overpopulation. Or any other problem, for that matter. All the great problems of our country and of our world have their roots in one thing: the vast majority of the people are spiritually stagnating and declining, and very few ascending. Everybody thinks they're a 'good person,' but hardly anyone is making daily progress in ascension, and that's what's really needed. Most have never experienced enough ascension to start believing that physical immortality might really be possible."

Acknowledging our physical immortality changes our outlook on life, it allows us to see seven generations into the future giving us more incentive to make a difference now. While many religions have people vying for the gates of heaven or figuring out what they want to be in their next life, physical immortals, like myself, understand that heaven on earth is the work which lies before us. And that work begins with taking care of ourselves and our children, a labor of love that will heal the other signifants in our lives as well.

A brighter tomorrow depends on the degree of illumination we give to the needs of today. By rolling up our sleeves and scrubbing sweet potatoes at the river's edge of life, we are saying YES to humanity's ascension into the creation of Heaven on Earth.

I believe in forever and, contrary to what has previously been embraced, life is not a one-night stand.

Appendix A:
When And How I Feed
My Fruitarian Family

I am often asked what constitutes a typical day in the dietary life of my fruitarian family. Because our meals are in alignment with our activities, I am offering a whole view of a given day at our Paradise Ranch where I happily raise my three children, write books, and manage our family business.

I leave the family bed at 4:00 am to begin writing while my children continue sleeping until around 7:00 am, at which time we all hop into the hot tub together with either a breakfast of fresh-squeezed citrus juice or a big bowl of watermelon. What a wonderful way to say HELLO! to a brand new day. After discussing our dreams from the night before, we get ready for a fun reading session.

Around 8:00 am we create a luscious fruit smoothie made from frozen banana pieces, soaked almond, soaked sunflower seeds, papaya, and water. After finishing this delightful meal we all head out into the still-cool of the morning where my children play and tend to their animals and other homeschooling responsibilities while I work on various writing projects and answer correspondence.

Between 9:00 am and 10:00 am I prepare a large mono-fruit platter of watermelon, canteloupe, honeydew, grapes, or whatever other juicy fruit sounds good to us. At this point, my children begin settling into one particular project such as sewing, mechanics, writing, carpentry, etc.

Around 1:00 pm I pack up my music selection (Amy Grant and Kenny G. are among my favorites), Walk-woman and earphones, resource material for the writing project at hand, and a basket filled with fruit as we head off to the beach or the pool for an afternoon of sunbathing, water-play, dance, yoga, and gymnastics. We stay long enough to catch the last drops of the sun's golden rays, then head home for a feast of papayas, passion fruit, or whatever else is ripe and in need of our culinary attention..

As Paradise on Earth makes its daily turn away from the sun, my family turns inward to the comforts of home. We celebrate the closing of another beautiful day in the same manner we began it...in the hot tub, only this time with fruit smoothie popsicles or apple halves with the center scooped out enough to fill with raw nutbutter. Sometimes we top off our day with an arts & crafts-like burrito party consisting of avocado slices, tomato wedges, peas, corn, sprouts, and fresh salsa wrapped into a lettuce leaf tortilla.

Our evening is about dancing to our favorite music, relishing in the memories made on this day, and discussing our dreams yet to be realized, determining what next steps are necessary for bringing those goals to fruition. Then we start migrating toward the family bed where we read soothing books, sing special songs, and give thanks for another wonderful day, spent together.

RESOURCES

Books To Grow By

The Alchemist, Paulo Coelho
***Anatomy Of An Accomplishment**, Hygeia Halfmoon
***As You Think**, James Allen
***Awakening Our Self-Healing Body**, Arthur M. Baker
***Blatant Raw-Foodist Propaganda**, Joe Alexander
Celestine Prophecy, James Redfield
Celestine Prophecy Experiential Guide, James Redfield
Codependent No More, Melody Beattie
Codependent Parent, Barbara Cottman Becnel
Continuum Concept, Jean Liedloff
***Cooked Foods Anonymous**, Hygeia Halfmoon
***Diet For A New America**, John Robbins
Drama Of The Gifted Child, Alice Miller
***Everyday Erotica For The Totally Devoted Couple**, Hygeia
  Halfmoon
The Education Of Little Tree, Forrest Carter
Family Bed, Tine Thevenin
Feel The Fear And Do It Anyway!, Susan Jeffers
***Fit For Life**, Marilyn and Harvey Diamond
***Fruitarian Diet And Physical Rejuvenation**, Dr. O.L.M.
  Abramowski
***Gaining Weight and Building Muscle & Strength On The
  Raw-Food Diet**, Stephen Arlin
***Highway To Health: A Call To Fruitarianism**, Hygeia
  Halfmoon
Hind's Feet On High Places, Hannah Hurnard

Hundredth Monkey, Ken Keyes
Illusions, Richard Bach
IS Philosophy, Stephen Arlin
Jonathan Livingston Seagull, Richard Bach
Live Your Dreams, Les Brown
***Love Letters**, Hygeia Halfmoon
Magical Child, Joseph Chilton Pearce
Nature Of Personal Reality, Jane Roberts
***Nature's First Law: The Raw-Food Diet**, Arlin-Dini-Wolfe
***On Form And Actuality**, David Wolfe
One Minute Mother, Spencer Johnson
Natural Superiority Of Women, Ashley Montagu
***A New Age Perspective On Art**, Joe Alexander
Precious Present, Spencer Johnson
The Prophet, Kahlil Gibran
***Prostitute To Ph.D.**, Hygeia Halfmoon
Punished By Rewards, Alfie Kohn
***Raw Courage World**, R.C. Dini
***Raw-Food Recipes: A Fruitarian Child's Delight!**,
   Halfmoon-Vanlaanen
Tao Of Motherhood, Vimala McClure
Think And Grow Rich, Napoleon Hill
Together Forever, Brown-BernaDeane-Strole
Unassisted Childbirth, Laura Kaplan Shanley
***Wealth Is the Answer**, Hygeia Halfmoon
Womanly Art Of Breastfeeding, La Leche League
You Can Heal Your Life, Louise Hay

*Books now available from: Nature's First Law
   1-800-205-2350

PUBLICATIONS

An Apple A Day, Hygeia's Newsletter!
Covers: Fruitarian Mothering * Natural Birth *
Breastfeeding * Postpartum Weight Loss * Cooked-food
Addiction Support * Lessons in Recovery * Nurturing
Children * Exercise, and more!
12 issues/year, $36/year.
800-205-2350

Compleat Mother magazine
PO Box 209 Minot, ND 58702 USA
701-852-2822
E-mail: jody@minot.com

Fruitarian Network News, (4 issues/year)
Support for Fruitarians world-wide.
Director: Rene Beresford * Regular Features:
International Contacts * Fruit Poetry * Self-Help
Information * Interviews * Fruit Facts.
$41/year. To subscribe write, call, or e-mail:
Nature's First Law
PO Box 900202, San Diego, CA 92190 USA
800-205-2350
E-mail: nature@io-online.com

Just Eat An Apple (6 issues/year)
From the Nature's First Law head office...
An uncomprising approach to the RAW lifestyle!
Editor: Frederic Patenaude * Regular Features:
Interviews * Food & Sex * Fascinating Raw Philosophy *
What's Raw, What's Cooked * What's Happening in The
Raw-Food World * Networking Contacts.
$30/year ($40/year foreign). 16 pages/issue.
To subscribe write, call, or e-mail:
Nature's First Law
PO Box 900202, San Diego, CA 92190 USA
800-205-2350
E-mail: nature@io-online.com

Letters From Home, Unassisted Childbirth
760 36th St., Boulder, CO 80303 USA
http://www.geocities.com/heartland/meadows/7535
303-444-5197

Living Nutrition magazine (4 issues/year)
The World's premier magazine dedicated to helping
health seekers learn how to succeed with eating our
natural diet of raw foods! Excellent format, high
quality, 32+ pages. Regular Features: Dietary
Transition Help * Physical Fitness Pointers *
Healthful Eating Guidelines * Networking Contacts *
Raw-Food Events * Raw-Food Recipes * Literature
Reviews * Natural Healing Education * Testimonials *
Biodynamic Organiculture Articles * Raw-Food
Parenting * Nature's First Law Column.
$20/1-year subscription (US$25 foreign),
$30/2-year subscription (US$40 foreign)
To subscribe write or call: Nature's First Law
PO Box 900202, San Diego, CA 92190 USA
800-205-2350

Mother Is Me
http://members.aol.com/zoey455/index.html
800-693-6852

Mothering magazine
PO Box 1690, Santa Fe, NM 87504 USA
505-984-8116

Nurturing Parent
3213 W Main St. Suite 153, Rapid City, SD 57702 USA
605-399-2990

ORGANIZATIONS

Nature's First Law: The Raw-Food Diet
The World's Premier Source of Raw-Food Diet
Books, Juicers, Booklets, Videos, and Audio Tapes.
PO Box 900202, San Diego, CA 92190 USA
http://www.rawfood.com
E-mail: nature@io-online.com
800-205-2350

Attachment Parenting, Children's Rights
1508 Clairmont Place, Nashville, TN 37215 USA
http://iquest.com/~parkers
615-298-4334

Dissatisfied Parents Together, Anti-Vaccination
512 W. Maple Ave #206, Vienna, VA 22180 USA
http://www.909shot.com
800-909-SHOT

Growing Without Schooling
Home-Based Education
2269 Massachusetts Ave., Cambridge, MA 02140 USA
617-864-3100

La Leche League, Breastfeeding Support
PO Box 4079, Schaumburg, IL 60168-4079 USA
847-519-7730

Les Brown Unlimited, Live Your Dreams!
PO Box 1646, Brighton, MI 48116 USA
313-961-1962

Loving Foods, Raw Experience Raw-Food Restaurant
Owners: Renee Underkoffler & Jeremy Safron
42 Baldwin Ave., Paia (Maui), HI 96779 USA
808-579-9729

Mother & Child Reunion, Primal Mothering Products!
The World's Best Baby Slings!
800-788-1740

NOCTRC, Stop Circumcision Now
PO Box 2512, San Anselmo, CA 94979-2512 USA

Parent's Resource Connection
5102 Deerwood Lane, NE Bemidji, MN 56601 USA
218-751-3136

People Forever, Physical Immortality Movement
PO Box 12305, Scotsdale, AZ 85267 USA

Raw Living Foods, Raw-Food Restaurant
Owner: Jeremy Safron
1224 9th Avenue, San Francisco, CA 94122 USA
415-665-6519

Seventh Generation, Healthy Home Products
360 Interlocken Blvd. #300, Broomfield, CO 80021 USA

Unassisted Childbirth Support Network
760 36th St., Boulder, CO 80303 USA
http://www.geocities.com/Heartland/Meadows/7535
E-mail: bornfree@ecentral.com
303-444-5197

The author and publisher wish to express thanks and appreciation to those listed below who granted permission to use the following material:

Dell, a division of Bantam, Doubleday, Dell Publishing Group Inc., for permission to quote from **Illusions**, **Jonathan Livingston Seagull** by Richard Bach and **I Could Do Anything** by Barbara Sher.

Houghton Mifflin Company for permission to quote from **Punished By Rewards** by Alfie Kohn.

Greenwood Publishing Group Inc. for permission to quote from **Unassisted Childbirth** by Laura K. Shanley.

Eleanor Friede Books, Inc. for permission to quote from **The Education Of Little Tree** by Forrest Carter.

New World Library for permission to quote from **Tao Of Motherhood** by Vimala McClure.

Parallax Press for permission to quote from **For A Future To Be Possible: Commentaries On The Five Mindfulness Trainings** by Thich Nhat Hanh.

The author and publisher made all reasonable efforts to contact all other literature sources quoted in the text.

Additional Copies of Primal Mothering

Additional copies of **Primal Mothering In A Modern World** may be ordered directly from Nature's First Law. One book is $14.95 plus $3.00 shipping and handling ($9.00 S&H if outside the United States or Canada). For each additional book please add only $1.00 shipping (add $6.00 S&H if outside the United States or Canada). California residents add 7.75% sales tax. Bulk discounts are available.

If you have any questions or comments about any of the material contained in this book, feel free to write, call, or e-mail Hygeia Halfmoon and/or Nature's First Law. We seek correspondence with all like-minded individuals seeking the glorious path to Paradise on Earth.

Also, check out the Nature's First Law Catalog. Each Catalog contains the highest-quality books, juicers, booklets, video tapes, and audio tapes on The Raw-Food Diet, Fruitarianism, and related material. To receive a free copy of the Nature's First Law Catalog please write, call, or e-mail Nature's First Law.

Nature's First Law
PO Box 900202
San Diego, CA 92190 U.S.A.
(619) 645-7282
(800) 205-2350 - orders only

E-mail: nature@io-online.com
Internet Homepage: http://www.rawfood.com